Mama Peggy's Recipes & Ruminations

a cookbook
by Peggy Chaney

edited and foreword
by Kevin Wicasta Lovelace

Copyright © 2018 by Windhaven Network, LLC

All rights reserved. No part of this publication may be reproduced, distributed, or transmitted in any form or by any means, including photocopying, recording, or other electronic or mechanical methods, without the prior written permission of the publisher, except in the case of brief quotations embodied in critical reviews and certain other noncommercial uses permitted by copyright law. For permission requests, write to the publisher, addressed "Attention: Permissions Coordinator," at the e-mail address below.

questions@windhavennetwork.com

Windhaven Network, LLC
Saint Petersburg, Florida
www.windhavennetwork.com

Printed in the United States of America

ISBN: 978-1-7322810-0-4 (Paperback)
Library of Congress Control Number: 2018905323

Publisher's Cataloging-in-Publication data
Chaney, Peggy.
Mama Peggy's Recipes & Ruminations: A Cookbook / Peggy Chaney; with Kevin Wicasta Lovelace.
p. cm.

1. American cooking — Southern style.

Founders' Edition, 2018

This work is dedicated to the memories of

Peggy Joyce Chaney
May 11, 1933 – Dec 30, 2011

Loretta Lee Chaney
Jan 4, 1935 – Jul 9, 2002

and

Peggy's Restaurant
Kings Mountain, North Carolina
(and all who ever worked there)

Table of Contents

Recipes
Main Dishes 9
Casseroles 41
Gravy 76
Appetizers 83
Beverages 98
Bread 108
Desserts – Cakes 117
Desserts – Candy & Cookies 145
Desserts – Pies 159
Desserts – Pudding and Other 186
Side Dishes 213
Soups & Stews 237
Dressing, Salads & Spreads 244

Ruminations from Peggy's Blog
Mama's Birthday 7
Dear Lo 39
In Church Again 74
You Can't Go Home Again! 81
A Drastic Decision 96
The Christmas Spirit 105
Happy New Year 114
Loretta, My Best Friend 140
Valentine's Day 156
Woodpecker! 184
Sunshine and Warm Weather 211
My Encounter 234
Christmas 241

Addendum
The Chaney Bunch 251
Peggy's Restaurant Menu 252
Index 256
My Recipes 264

FOUNDERS – A NOTE

Mama Peggy's Recipes & Ruminations was made possible, in part, by the support of all of the amazing people who visited the web site at MamaPeggy.com and supported the Facebook page with much love and encouragement – amazing people who were willing to pre-order the cookbook before it was even printed! We will always be in their debt, and they will always be in our hearts. Without their support, this cookbook might not have happened at all.

Those people will be listed in all future editions of this work as The Founders in this space. We wish we could have listed them here, but it simply wasn't possible, since we had to order the books prior to the publication date to have them ready. I still wanted to set aside a space where they will know where their names can be found in future editions.

~ Kevin Wicasta Lovelace

Introduction

One of the things which slowed the publication of this cookbook was the writing of this introduction. I've started, and abandoned, it many times. The problem was simple. How does one write an introduction for their mother? How do you sum up the life of someone who gave *you* life? There are no guidelines for that. Most of us think our mothers are amazing. At least in retrospect. Maybe we don't think that so much when we're young and think we know everything. But as we get older and face down our own struggles, most of us eventually realize what a hard road our mothers traveled, and how much we were shielded from the harsh realities of a hard world.

Okay, I admit that not all of us may have had the ideal childhood, and some of us grew up with issues. But if there is one thing I always knew about my mother, it was that she always on my side. But it wasn't just me. Everyone who knew Peggy Chaney knew that she was on their side. Her spirit was a bright, shining example of what a beautiful soul looked like, and everyone who knew Mama loved her. As one of my cousins, Jerry Millwood, a Baptist preacher, said at Mama's funeral service, "her life was her testament". Nothing else needs to be said, really.

So… we've established that Mama was a good person. How does this translate to a cookbook?

It's simple. One of the most common ways Mama had of expressing her love was through her cooking. Mama loved cooking for people. It was her gift, and she was very good at it. But more than that, she loved sharing that gift with others.

Whether at work in our family's "café", Peggy's Restaurant, which she ran with her sister, Loretta, for over 20 years in Kings Mountain, North Carolina, or in her apartment where she lived out her final years, Mama believed in feeding people. I'm reminded of an elderly gentleman who talked to me during the visitation after Mama died in 2011. He told me, "Your mother fed everybody in this town at one time or another [he meant at the restaurant]. There's some of her in every one of us." Another man, a young one, shared with me his memories of eating at Peggy's Restaurant with his father and grandfather, and told me, "her cooking was a part of three generations of my family".

Cooking was a part of who my mother was. You couldn't separate one from the other. I still have cousins who check in and almost invariably say something about how much they miss her biscuits, or her gravy, or one thing or another that she used to cook. Food was at the center of Mama's being. She read cookbooks like other people read novels, and when she found one she thought sounded tasty, she would pick up the phone and call, and read you the entire recipe. I can still hear her. "Doesn't that sound good?" She had cooked for so long, she could almost taste the recipe just by reading it. The rest of us had to wait for her try her hand at it.

Clearly, I could go on for a while. When it comes to my mother, there are so many wonderful memories. It's hard to pick out just a few. But that's not what an introduction is about, is it? This is where I'm supposed to tell what you'll find in the pages that follow. I think a lot of that has already been summed up in the title, though. "Mama Peggy's Recipes & Ruminations". That's what's here.

I'll sum up a little background, and then we can move on to the good stuff. Naturally, you'll find plenty of recipes here. This isn't, by any means, a comprehensive collection of Mama's recipes. I had to leave a lot of stuff out. There are boxes upstairs in my home full of hand-written recipes and notes. But this all started out as an effort to help Mama put together a cookbook. That was always her dream. Which, of course, makes sense. For a cook, leaving behind recipes is a way of leaving behind a part of yourself. The problem where Mama was concerned was that we had a hard time getting her to put down her own recipes. She was more eager to share good recipes she had come across, and she shared a lot on the MamaPeggy.com web site. I had to recreate some of her signature dishes by trial and error, drawing upon years of working in the kitchen with her at Peggy's Restaurant. In that regard, I was lucky to have soaked up a lot more of how she did things than I realized at the time. The one thing which kept me on the path, and helped me uncover some of those recipes, was reminding myself of something Mama always said when I asked her for details about this recipe or that. She would say, "Lord, it's the simplest thing in the world." When I approached recipes from that perspective, of someone who was just trying to cook a good meal for their hungry family, that's when those recipes finally came together.

That's all Mama's cooking was. Good eating. She wasn't trying to show off or impress anyone with her presentation. This was about being hungry and eating good food. It really was "the simplest thing in the world".

I believe that's the lasting appeal of these recipes. On the web site and in private messages, so many people have told me the recipes on MamaPeggy.com (most can be found in these pages) were the kinds of food that their grandmother or mother used to make. So many times, people thanked us for letting them taste their grandmother's biscuits again. The most popular recipe on the web site, by far, was (and still is) the stewed potatoes recipes. That's a great metaphor for all these recipes, really. You can't get more basic than a recipe which is little more than potatoes, some bacon grease, and a little flour. But people can't get enough of it. There's some part of all of us, especially those of us who were raised in the South, that isn't about cooking competitions on cable TV, or pretending our dishes could be served in a fancy, upscale restaurant. Some of us want the kind of food you'd find at a family reunion in North or South Carolina, or being brought to a grieving family in Georgia after the passing of a loved one, or being served around a family's holiday table at Thanksgiving or Christmas in Tennessee. Just good, simple, filling food, for people with empty bellies who look forward to sharing a meal with friends and family.

The simplest thing in the world.

I can still see Mama sitting in the living room or her apartment, rocking in that chair, slowly flipping through the pages as she plowed through one of her favorite old cookbooks. If ever anyone deserved to have a cookbook of her own, it was Mama. And now she has it.

I may have finished this cookbook for her. But Mama started it. This is her cookbook, and no one else's. In fact, it being *her* cookbook is one of the only things which sets it apart from countless others. As I've said, these aren't fancy recipes. These are the types of recipes which mothers, sons, daughters, and grandmothers are cooking across Southern states as we speak. It's not "a Southern thing", though. If you're from up North or "out West", your family will love these recipes as much as anyone else. But there's a definite Southern flavor to a lot of them. Make of that what you will.

Anyway, I've rambled on long enough. Mama used to say that no one could talk as much as me once I got rolling. She's right. And where the subject of my mother, Peggy Chaney, goes, I could talk all night. I miss her so much.

In closing, I'll just say what I probably should have said in the first paragraph. This cookbook probably began in the kitchen at the Minute Grill, where Mama, Loretta, and some of my other aunts, worked once upon a time. Or maybe at the Silver Villa. Or Bob's Café (which Mama ran with my father for a time). But it was born in the kitchen at Peggy's Restaurant, which it should always be connected to. If you ever ate at Peggy's, you'll know what I mean.

The design idea which this cookbook followed was that it should be kept as simple as possible, like all those old community cookbooks you could buy from churches and in community organizations in small towns all across America. I wanted this cookbook to be useful. This is not a cookbook you park on your coffee table to impress your neighbors. This one should be kept in the kitchen, within reach.

Each section is prefaced with one of Mama's posts from her web site. That's the "Ruminations" part in the title. There hopefully aren't too many. I just didn't see a way to put together Mama's cookbook without including her wit, humor, and shining examples of love. Hopefully somewhere among these pages you'll get a sense for who Peggy Chaney was, and why so many people thought she needed her own cookbook. You'll also find in Mama's writings references to her sisters and brothers (she was one of eleven children who grew up during the Great Depression, children of a Baptist preacher), as well as other people she knew. I haven't tried to explain who everyone is. Mama often explains that. But if she doesn't explain, it doesn't change the context of what she wrote about.

The last thing I'll say is to point out that we printed this cookbook in a slightly larger format than usual. Many of our older friends expressed interest in the cookbook, and we wanted them to be able to use it without having to strain to read it. Younger folks might also find that the larger font size helps in the kitchen, as you're leaning over from the bowl into which you're cracking eggs, to make sure of the next step of the meal you're cooking for your family. Mama would have wanted it to be easy to read, too, because it's about being useful, not about being seen.

I hope you find in these pages something useful. And I hope Mama Peggy's spirit hangs out with you in the kitchen, like I sometimes feel she does with me. If you ever find yourself wondering if something needs a bit more salt, or some pepper, just ask, "Mama, what do you think?" Sure, it could just be my imagination, but whenever I do, I always seem to make the right choice. If ever there was anything Mama might visit us to help with, it would be us cooking in the kitchen.

I hope Mama hangs out with you, as well.

Thank you for being here.

Kevin Wicasta Lovelace
a.k.a. "Peggy's son"

Peggy's Blog – Mama's Birthday
February 8, 2002

Today is Mama's birthday. She has been gone for over 35 years and there is still times that I miss her so bad and would just give anything if I could have one of those talks we used to have. Somehow Mama could always make things right. She seemed to be able to just look at us and know what was going on with us. She also believed in prayer.

I remember the time I had a date with a very handsome fella and Mama started praying (she told me about it later on) because she had misgivings about him. She said she told God that if he wasn't the right kind of fellow, to keep him from coming that night.

Well, needless to say, he didn't show up for our date, and to tell you the truth I never did even know what happened to him. I never saw nor heard from him again.

I wonder if she knows what is going on with Sis?

Sis is sleeping this morning. She seems to feel read bad, too! I wish I understood more about this cancer so I could know what is happening day by day.

My prayer has been that God would help me to be able to be there for her every step of the way and to help her to know how much I love her.

I pray that when the time comes and He calls her home that He will just reach down and scoop her up into His loving arms and that angels will surround her.

Mama and Daddy will be waiting for her. So will Lucille, Grady, Robert and Johnny.

Can't you just imagine the thrill of seeing Jesus at last, face to face? And then seeing the smiles on the faces of our loved ones? Glory to God!!!

Main Dishes

Baked Chicken Breasts

A moist and tender chicken dish.

Ingredients

- 4 Skinless Chicken Breasts
- 1 cup Dukes Mayonnaise
- ¼ cup mustard
- 1 pkg. Pepperidge Farm Dressing Mix

Instructions

1. Make a mixture of mayonnaise and mustard.
2. Roll chicken breasts into mayonnaise and mustard mixture.
3. Roll chicken into dressing mix.
4. Place breasts on pan lined with aluminum foil.
5. Bake at 325 degrees for 30 - 60 minutes depending on size of chicken breasts.

Recipe type: Main Dish
Serves: 4
Prep time: 10 mins
Cook time: 40 mins
Total time: 50 mins

Basic Best Salmon Loaf

A great, old-fashioned salmon loaf recipe.

Ingredients

- 1 can (14.75 oz.) Double Q Alaskan Salmon
- 2 cups soft bread crumbs
- ⅓ cup finely minced onions
- ¼ cup milk
- 2 eggs
- 2 Tbsp. minced parsley
- 1 Tbsp. lemon juice
- ¼ tsp. salt
- ¼ tsp. dill weed
- dash pepper

Instructions

1. Drain Salmon, reserve 2 Tbsp. liquid; flake.
2. Combine all ingredients.
3. Place in well-greased 8½ by 4½ by 2½ loaf pan or shape into loaf on greased baking pan.
4. Bake at 350 degrees for 45 minutes.
5. For Salmon Patties: Prepare salmon mixture as above. Shape into eight 1-inch thick patties. Pan-fry on both sides in 2 Tbsp. oil or butter until golden brown.

Recipe type: Main Dish
Serves: 6
Prep time: 15 mins
Cook time: 45 mins
Total time: 1 hour

CROUTON BREADED CHICKEN

This hand-written recipe was found scribbled down in one of Mama Peggy's notebooks.

Ingredients

- 2 (4 oz.) boneless skinless chicken breasts (pounded to ½-inch thickness)
- ⅓ cup reduced fat buttermilk
- Olive oil in spray bottle (not from grocery store that contains propellant)
- 1 oz. fat free croutons

Instructions

1. Put chicken in medium resealable plastic bag.
2. Pour buttermilk over and seal the bag. Let soak 6 hours or overnight.
3. Preheat oven to 450 degrees.
4. Lightly mist a small, non-stick pan or sheet with spray.
5. Add the croutons to a plastic bag. Pound them with the flat side of a mallet until crush very fine.
6. Put the crumbs into a shallow bowl.

7. Remove chicken breast from the bag and let excess drip off. Dip it into crumbs, rotating it to cover the breast completely.
8. Place breaded breast onto the prepared sheet so that breasts don't touch.
9. If crumbs remain, press them into top of remaining breasts.
10. Lightly spray top of breasts with spray.
11. Bake for 5 minutes and then carefully, being sure not to remove the coating, flip them.
12. Lightly mist the tops with spray and continue to bake for 3 to 5 minutes more or until the coating is crisp and chicken is no longer pink inside.
13. Serve immediately.

Recipe type: Main Dish
Serves: 4
Prep time: 6 hours
Cook time: 20 mins
Total time: 6 hours 20 mins

Chicken & Dumplings
(My sister Edith's recipe)

A wonderful recipe for home-made chicken & dumplings.

Ingredients

- 1 hen or 4 large chicken breasts (do not remove skin)
- 1 stick of margarine
- Seasoning; salt and pepper
- 4 cups plain flour, sifted

Instructions

1. Cook chicken in large pot (cover chicken with water) until well done. Let cool.
2. Remove chicken from pot. Shred and save until later.
3. Pour 2 cups cooled broth into bed of flour to form dough.
4. Divide dough into several pieces and roll out with rolling pin.
5. Cut dough into strips.
6. Reheat broth in pot to rolling boil.
7. Add margarine (or butter) and allow to melt.
8. Drop dumplings into boiling broth. Let boil 5 to 10 minutes.

9. Put shredded chicken back into pot and boil 5 minutes more.

"I love boiled, sliced eggs in mine, added last, before serving." ~ *Mama Peggy*

Editor's Note: This is how they made chicken and dumplings in the old days. This recipe was shared with Mama Peggy by her sister, Edith Chaney Millwood.

Recipe type: Main Dish
Serves: 6
Prep time: 45 mins
Cook time: 15 mins
Total time: 1 hour

QUICK CHICKEN AND DUMPLINGS (PEGGY'S RESTAURANT WAY)

Ingredients

- 1 large hen or 4 large chicken breasts
- 2 cans Campbell's cream of chicken soup
- 1 lg. pkg. of Mueller's dumplings
- 3 or 4 eggs (Boiled and sliced)
- 1 stick of margarine

Instructions

1. Cook chicken or chicken breasts in pot, covered with water.
2. Salt and pepper to taste.

3. Cook until done and dip chicken out.
4. Cool chicken and then shred.
5. Strain broth and put back into pot.
6. Add two cans of Cream of Chicken soup and margarine.
7. Then add shredded chicken.
8. Stir and bring to rolling boil.
9. Then stir in dumplings.
10. Turn off heat. Close lid tightly. Do not be tempted to check on them. Let sit for about an hour.
11. Then add boiled and sliced eggs.

"None of our customers at Peggy's Restaurant seemed to care that the dumplings were made with pasta dumplings. In fact, we sold the heck out of those dumplings. On Fridays we had standing room only. I would not let anything that I prepared go out of that kitchen until it tasted *just* right to me. Of course, we won't talk about the problem I had keeping my weight under control!!!!!!!. The pot I used held 12 chickens so you can imagine how much I prepared for the cafe. WHEW!!!!!!" ~ *Mama Peggy*

Recipe type: Main Dish
Serves: 6
Prep time: 15 mins
Cook time: 1 hour
Total time: 1 hour 15 mins

Chicken Lickin' Pork Chops

Ingredients

- 6-8 pork chops, 1 - thick.
- ½ cup of flour
- 1 Tbsp. salt
- 1½ tsp. dry mustard
- ½ tsp. garlic powder
- 2 Tbsp. oil
- 1 can chicken and rice soup

Instructions

1. Dredge pork chops in mixture of flour, salt, dry mustard, and garlic powder.
2. Brown in oil in large skillet.
3. Place browned pork chops in crock-pot.
4. Add can of soup.
5. Cover and cook on Low for 6-8 hours or on High for 3 ½ hours.
6. Delicious!

"My Late sister Dot 'Sis' (as we called her) brought this recipe to me when she lived in Atlanta. It is really good!"
~ *Mama Peggy*

Recipe type: Main Dish
Serves: 8
Prep time: 20 mins
Cook time: 6 hours
Total time: 6 hours 20 mins

Creamy Cheese Grits and Spinach

Ingredients

- 1 (5 oz.) package of baby spinach, thoroughly washed
- 1 ½ cups vegetable broth
- 1 cup quick cooking grits
- 1 cup 2% reduced fat milk
- ½ tsp. salt
- ⅛ tsp. garlic powder
- ½ (8 oz.) package shredded mozzarella-provolone cheese blend

Instructions

1. Coarsely chop spinach.
2. Bring grits to a boil in a medium saucepan over medium-high heat.
3. Reduce heat to low, and simmer, stirring occasionally, 10 to 12 minutes or until thickened.
4. Stir in spinach and cheese until well blended and cheese is melted.
5. Serve immediately.

Recipe type: Main Dishes
Serves: 4-6
Prep time: 10 mins
Cook time: 15 mins
Total time: 25 mins

Crock Pot Beef Stew

This is a scrumptious beef stew recipe you can make in your crock pot when you don't have time to linger in the kitchen. Just throw the ingredients in the crock pot and let it simmer while you take care of the rest of your day.

Ingredients

- 3 carrots, cut up
- 3 potatoes, cut up
- 2 lbs. beef chuck or stew meat
- 1 cup of water or beef stock
- 1 tsp. Worcestershire sauce
- 1 clove garlic (optional)
- 1 bay lead (optional)
- 1 Tbsp. salt
- ½ tsp. pepper
- 1 tsp. paprika (optional)
- 3 onions, quartered
- 1 stalk celery, cut up (optional)

Instructions

1. Put all of the ingredients in your crock pot in the order listed.
2. Stir just enough to mix the spices.
3. Cover and set to low for 10 to 12 hours or high for 5 to 6 hours.

Recipe type: Main Dish
Serves: 8
Prep time: 15 mins
Cook time: 10 hours
Total time: 10 hours 15 mins

CROCK-POT CHICKEN

Ingredients

- 3 lb. chicken, cut up into pieces
- 1 tsp. salt
- 1 tsp. pepper
- 1 can cream of mushroom soup
- ½ cup sweet wine or sherry
- 2 Tbsp. butter
- 2 Tbsp. Italian dressing mix, dry
- 1 Tbsp. chopped onion
- 6 oz. cream cheese, cut into cubes

Instructions

1. Wash chicken and pat dry.
2. Brush with butter.
3. Sprinkled with salt and pepper.
4. Place in crockpot.
5. Sprinkle with dry salad mix.
6. Cover and cook on low for 5-6 hours.
7. About 45 minutes before serving, mix soup, cream cheese, wine and onion in small saucepan. Cook until smooth.

8. Pour mixture over chicken in crockpot.
9. Cover and cook for 30 minutes on low.
10. Serve with sauce, with rice or noodles.

Recipe type: Main Dishes, Casserole
Serves: 4 - 6
Prep time: 15 mins
Cook time: 6 hours 30 mins
Total time: 6 hours 45 mins

FRESH CORN CAKES

Ingredients

- 2 ½ cups fresh corn (About 5 ears)
- 3 large eggs
- ¾ cup milk
- 3 Tbsp. butter, melted
- ¾ cup plain flour
- ¾ cup corn meal
- 1 (8 oz.) pkg. fresh mozzarella cheese, grated
- 2 Tbsp. chopped chives
- 1 tsp. salt
- 1 tsp. pepper

Instructions

1. Pulse first 4 ingredients in food processor 3 to 4 times or just until corn is coarsely chopped.
2. Stir together flour and next 5 ingredients in a large bowl.

3. Stir in corn just until dry ingredients are moistened.
4. Spoon ½ cup batter for each cake onto a hot and lightly greased griddle or a large nonstick pan, to form 2-inch cakes.
5. Do not spread or flatten cakes.
6. Cook cakes 3 to 4 minutes or until tops are covered with bubbles and edges look cooked.
7. Turn and cook other side.

Recipe type: Main Dish
Serves: 6
Prep time: 30 mins
Cook time: 20 mins
Total time: 50 mins

FRIED CHICKEN STRIPS

Ingredients

- 3 lb. chicken, cut into strips
- 4 Tbsp. flour
- 2 tsp. salt
- ½ cup lemon juice
- 2 Tbsp. softened butter
- 1½ cup Bisquick mix
- 1 tsp. paprika
- ½ tsp. sage
- ¼ tsp. pepper
- 1 cup milk
- 24 oz. vegetable oil

Instructions

1. Wipe chicken dry.
2. Combine flour, lemon juice, salt, and butter into a paste.
3. Coat chicken evenly.
4. Put coated pieces into a bowl.
5. Combine Bisquick mix with spice.
6. Dip chicken pieces into milk and then into mixture. Dust off excess.
7. In large skillet, heat oil until bubbling slightly.
8. Fry chicken pieces until lightly browned (about 4 minutes on each side).
9. Place chicken in shallow pan and spoon any remaining milk over pieces,
10. Seal with foil, and bake at 350 degrees for 1 hour.
11. Uncover and baste with milk again.
12. Bake for 10 minutes at 400 degrees, uncovered, to crisp the chicken.

Recipe type: Main Dish
Serves: 8
Prep time: 15 mins
Cook time: 1 hour 10 mins
Total time: 1 hour 25 mins

MY MAMA'S SALMON PATTIES

Ingredients

- 1 lg. can of pink salmon
- 1 egg, beaten
- ¼ cup cornmeal
- ¼ cup flour
- ½ cup buttermilk
- ½ tsp. salt
- ⅛ tsp. pepper
- Cooking oil

Instructions

1. Remove bones and skin from salmon; crumble fine.
2. Mix all ingredients, stirring well.
3. Shape like patties with your hands or drop by Tbsp. into hot cooking oil.
4. Brown on both sides.
5. Drain on paper towels.

"Simple but delicious! I have a very funny story about my sweet sister, Lucille and frying salmon patties that I will post later." ~ *Mama Peggy*

Recipe type: Main Dish
Serves: 6
Prep time: 15 mins
Cook time: 20 mins
Total time: 35 mins

OLD FASHIONED MEATLOAF

The beauty of a great meat loaf is often its simplicity, and Mama Peggy's meatloaf was legendary. That's the hallmark of good, Southern cooking, and this old-fashioned recipe is a perfect example.

Ingredients

- 2 lb. ground beef
- 2 eggs
- 1 medium onion, chopped
- ½ bell pepper, chopped
- 3 biscuits, crumbled
- ¼ cup milk
- ½ cup ketchup
- 2 tsp. Worcestershire sauce

Instructions

1. Combine all ingredients, mixing well.
2. Shape into a loaf.
3. Bake at 350 for one hour.
4. Remove and cover top with ketchup and bake for 20 more minutes.

Editor's Note: This nearly lost recipe was recovered with the assistance of Victoria Sadler Lovelace.

Recipe type: Main Dish
Serves: 6
Prep time: 10 mins
Cook time: 1 hour 20 mins
Total time: 1 hour 30 mins

OLD FASHIONED ROAST TURKEY

A classic, old-fashioned roast turkey recipe. If you want to cook a turkey like Grandma used to cook, this is a good way to do it. This goes well with our easy Chicken Gravy recipe!

Ingredients

- 14 to 16 lb. ready-to-cook turkey.
- 1 cup butter, melted
- salt
- pepper

Instructions

1. Remove giblets and neck from the turkey.
2. Wash and set them aside.
3. Wash the turkey inside and out, and then dry with paper towels.
4. Remove and discard the excess fat.
5. Preheat oven to 325 degrees (F).
6. Spoon some dressing into the neck cavity.
7. Bring skin of neck over the back, then fasten into place with a poultry pin.

8. Spoon the remaining dressing into the body cavity (don't pack it).
9. Insert 4 or 5 poultry pins at regular intervals, and lace the cavity closed with twine.
10. Bend the wing tips under the body and tie the ends of the legs together.
11. Insert a meat thermometer into the inside of a thigh at the thickest part.
12. Place the turkey in a shallow roasting pan and place into your oven.
13. Brush the top with some of the butter.
14. Sprinkle with salt and pepper.
15. Roast the turkey, uncovered, and brush it occasionally with the remaining butter and pan drippings.
16. When your turkey begins to turn golden, cover it with loose foil, and cook it for about 4½ hours, or until the thermometer registers 185 degrees F.
17. You're getting there when the leg joint moves freely.
18. Place the turkey on a heated platter.
19. Remove the twin and pins.
20. Let the turkey stand for about 20 minutes and serve!

Recipe type: Main Dish
Serves: 12
Prep time: 20 mins
Cook time: 4 hours 50 mins
Total time: 5 hours 10 mins

Pepper Steak

While it's not specifically a Southern thing, you'd find pepper steak on a lot of plates in the South. It's such a quick, easy dish that no recipe collection is complete without it.

Ingredients

- 2 lbs. round steak in ½-inch strips
- 3 Tbsp. oil
- 1 medium onion, sliced
- ¼ cup soy sauce
- ¼ cup sugar
- 1 tsp. salt
- 1 tsp. pepper
- ¼ tsp. ginger
- 2 green peppers, cut in strips
- 4 tomatoes, quartered
- ¼ cup water
- 1 Tbsp. cornstarch

Instructions

1. Brown the strip of round steak in oil.
2. Add the onion, soy sauce, sugar, seasonings, green pepper, tomatoes and water.
3. Cook for 15 minutes.
4. Mix the cornstarch with a little water and add.
5. Cook for 5 minutes.
6. Serve as-is or over some rice.

Recipe type: Main Dish
Serves: 4
Prep time: 10 mins
Cook time: 20 mins
Total time: 30 mins

Salisbury Steak

A favorite from Peggy's Restaurant. This recipe is a little different from what we did at the cafe, but not very. We didn't use spicy mustard in our Salisbury steak at Peggy's Restaurant, but it adds a little zing that works well at home.

Ingredients

- 1 lb. ground beef
- 1 tsp. onion salt
- ¼ tsp. pepper
- 1 Tbsp. vegetable oil
- 1 onion, finely chopped
- 2 Tbsp. unsalted butter
- 3 Tbsp. plain flour
- 2 cups beef stock
- 1 cup water
- 2 tsp. spicy mustard
- 2 tsp. Worcestershire sauce

Instructions

1. Add onion to a pan and cook in oil for about 2 minutes until onions are translucent.

2. Remove half of the onions into a large bowl (to make room for your beef).
3. Mix the ground beef, onion salt, and pepper.
4. Make patties and roll them in flour.
5. Place your patties in a pan and brown both sides (you don't have to cook them through and through. They'll finished cooking in the gravy you'll make next).
6. Remove the patties, put them on a plate, and set aside.
7. Reduce the pan to low heat and add butter.
8. Once your butter has melted, whisk in the 3 Tbsp. flour, beef stock, water, spicy mustard, and Worcestershire sauce until smooth.
9. Increase the heat to medium.
10. Stir the ingredients, add in the onions you set aside earlier, then add the steaks into the gravy (along with any juices that pooled on the plate).
11. Cook for 5-10 minutes, or until your gravy thickens and steaks are cooked through.
12. If your gravy thickens too fast, just add more water.
13. When your gravy is just about the right thickness, remove the steaks and put them back onto a plate.
14. Taste your gravy, salt and pepper to taste (when it's perfect, you'll know).
15. Now just serve up your Salisbury steaks, topped with your delicious gravy!

Recipe type: Main Dish
Serves: 4 – 5
Prep time: 15 mins
Cook time: 20 mins
Total time: 35 mins

SLOW COOKED BARBECUE PORK

A great, simple, slow-cooked barbecue pork recipe which will leave your house smelling like Heaven for most of the day! This makes great sandwiches with some slaw, or enjoy it as-is with some potato salad and sweet tea.

Ingredients

- 4 to 5 lbs. pork roast
- 1½ cup water
- ½ cup ketchup
- 1 cup vinegar
- ½ cup Worcestershire sauce
- 1 large onion
- 3 tsp. red pepper
- ¼ tsp. black pepper
- 1 tsp. salt

Instructions

1. Combine all ingredients in a crock pot.
2. Cook for 10 to 12 hours on low.
3. Remove pork from crock pot and allow to cool.
4. Pull pork apart and place into a large bowl.
5. Add leftover drippings to bowl and stir.
6. Makes great sandwiches with slaw!

Recipe type: Main Dish
Serves: 10 – 12
Prep time: 15 mins
Cook time: 12 hours
Total time: 12 hours 15 mins

SOUTHERN STEWED POTATOES

If you were raised in the South, you grew up eating stewed potatoes at least a couple of times a month, if not every week. Served with cornbread and black-eyed peas, stewed potatoes were a real treat from any proper old Southerner's childhood. And, to our friends up North, no, this is not a kind of potato soup.

Ingredients

- 6-8 large potatoes (peeled and cubed, about 1-inch cubes)
- salt and pepper
- 2 Tbsp. bacon grease (optional)
- 1 pinch onion flakes
- 2 Tbsp. flour
- ½ cup water
- ½ cup milk
- 3 Tbsp. butter

Instructions

1. Peel and cube the potatoes, put in a medium pot and fill with water until it's about 2 inches above potatoes.
2. Bring to a boil (you want the potatoes cooked until they are just fork tender, not falling apart.
3. After the potatoes are done, keep them in the same water you cooked them in and reduce to a low heat.

4. Put the flour and half cup of water in a bowl and blend with a whisk until the flour is dissolved.
5. Stirring constantly, but carefully, add the dissolved flour and water into the pot with the potatoes and water. Allow a few minutes to cook on simmer so that it can thicken.
6. Add more flour if you want it thicker, or more water if you want it thinner.
7. Add milk, salt, pepper, onion flakes and butter or bacon grease (if desired - it's fine without the bacon grease). Season to taste.

Editor's Note: This is easily the most popular recipe on the MamaPeggy.com web site.

Recipe type: Main Dish
Serves: 8
Prep time: 20 mins
Cook time: 35 mins
Total time: 55 mins

MamaPeggy.com Comments

"I have been looking for a long time to get a stewed potatoes recipe so that I could make potatoes like my grandmother almost 50 years ago and I think I just found it! Thank you SO much!! Can't wait to try to make this myself." ~ *Susan*

"I tried this yesterday. I loved this when I was a kid growing up in Kentucky. My wife had never had it. My Mom told me it was the best she'd ever had, and my wife loved it too. Thank you for such a good, sound recipe for an old favorite dish. I really appreciate it." ~ *Mark*

"The lady that babysat me after kindergarten, before Mamma came and picked me up from work, used to make this. I was only 3 or 4 but I have thought about this food since them. And I had the cornbread with them too. As soon as I saw the picture, I recognized it. Then when I read on and saw 'cornbread' it all came back to me. I couldn't believe it! You don't know how special that time was and how much I loved that dish. I thought it was something she came up to feed me that was simple and easy or something. I did not know that a recipe existed! I am so happy now. Talk about comfort food! Thank you very very much!" ~ *Lois R. Nesmith*

SPINACH LASAGNA ROLL-UPS

Ingredients

- 14 uncooked Lasagna noodles
- 1 large onion (finely chopped)
- 2 tsp. olive oil
- 2 garlic cloves, minced
- 3 & ½ Tbsp. all-purpose flour
- 3 & ½ cups 1% low fat milk
- 1 & ¾ tsp. salt, divided
- ½ tsp. freshly ground pepper, divided
- ⅛ tsp. ground nutmeg
- 1 (16 oz.) bag frozen cut leaf spinach, thawed
- 1 (24 oz.) small curd cottage cheese
- 1 cup grated part skim mozzarella cheese
- 1 large egg
- ¼ cup freshly grated Parmesan cheese

Instructions

1. Cook 7 lasagna noodles according to the package directions.
2. Remove with tongs or a slotted spoon to a large bowl of cold water.
3. Repeat with remaining noodles.
4. Drain noodles and arrange in a single layer on clean paper towels.
5. Cover with plastic wrap.
6. Cook onions in hot oil in a saucepan over medium heat, stirring occasionally, 8 minutes or until onion is caramel colored.

7. Add garlic, and sauté 1 minute. Reserve ¼ cup onion mixture.
8. Whisk flour into remaining onion mixture in saucepan, and cook, whisking constantly, 1 minute.
9. Gradually whisk in milk.
10. Cook over medium heat whisking constantly, 8 to 10 minutes or until sauce is thickened and bubbly.
11. Remove from heat; stir in ¾ tsp. salt, ¼ tsp. pepper, and ⅛ tsp. nutmeg.
12. Spoon ½ cup sauce into lightly greased 13 x 9-inch baking dish.
13. Drain spinach well, pressing between paper towels.
14. Preheat oven to 425 degrees.
15. Stir together spinach, cottage cheese, mozzarella cheese, egg, reserved ¼ cup onion mixture, and remaining 1 tsp. salt and ¼ tsp. pepper.
16. Spread about 3 Tbsp. spinach mixture over 1 noodle; roll up firmly and place, seam side down, in prepared baking dish.
17. Repeat with remaining noodles and spinach mixture.
18. Spoon remaining sauce over roll-ups and sprinkle with Parmesan cheese.
19. Bake at 425 degrees for 20 to 25 minutes or until golden and bubbly.
20. Let stand 5 minutes before serving.

"This is one of those recipes that you might not think you'll like until you try it. But once you do, you'll be glad you did!" ~ *Mama Peggy*

Recipe type: Main Dish
Serves: 6
Prep time: 20 mins
Cook time: 25 mins
Total time: 45 mins

STUFFED BELL PEPPERS

A classic American dish (and a Peggy's Restaurant favorite) that you don't often find in restaurants (unless it is a cafeteria) is stuffed bell peppers. They are basically a sort of meat mixture stuffed into bell peppers and baked in the oven. Done right, they'll make your mouth water.

Ingredients

- 1 lb. ground beef
- 1 medium onion, chopped
- 2 cups cooked rice
- ½ tsp. garlic salt
- ¼ tsp. salt
- ¼ tsp. pepper
- 1 15 oz. can tomato sauce
- 5 large green bell peppers
- 1 cup shredded Cheddar cheese (optional)

Instructions

1. Brown ground beef in skillet, stirring until crumbly; drain.
2. Add onion, rice, garlic salt, salt, pepper and half the tomato sauce.
3. Mix well.
4. Slice tops from peppers; discard seeds.
5. Spoon ground beef mixture into peppers.
6. Place in baking dish.
7. Top with cheese (if desired) and remaining tomato sauce.
8. Bake, covered, at 375 degrees for 50 minutes.

Recipe type: Main Dish
Serves: 5
Prep time: 20 mins
Cook time: 50 mins
Total time: 1 hour 10 mins

Peggy's Blog – Dear Lo
July 9th, 2003

Dear Lo,

Well, Honey, I've made it a whole year without you. I remember so well this day last year when I walked into your bedroom and found that you had left without me. God had reached down and picked you up and took you home to be with him. But you forgot someone! You forgot me!! I didn't think I would ever make this past year but God, in his goodness & mercy, has been with me and held me together.

It has been tough! I see you in so many ways and things every day. By the way, our fish died soon after you did. I haven't had the heart to try to get more. Oh! My! How you loved those fish! Enough to lay down on the ground that cold, cold day to try to get something that had fallen in that pond.

Remember the day your breast enhancer (falsie to most of us) fell in the pond when you stooped over to feed the fish! My, how we laughed at that.

We had so much fun together, didn't we? We didn't need anyone but just the two of us. We were satisfied to sit in that house and watch T.V. or piddle in the backyard. When you were able, you used to pick up all the mess I dug up. And my how well you "dead headed" those orange lilies that belong to Mama so they would keep blooming. I remember year before last when I put out those tomatoes and bell-peppers, how you would go out there with that towel and gather those tomatoes like we had struck gold or something! Ha ha

I miss you, Lo, and I long with all my heart to be with you and Sis and the rest of our family. Tell Sis I miss her, too, and that I loved her so much. More than she ever realized. Teresa & her family misses her too!

I feel like God took you first for a reason. I think I've realized that I had 3 more sisters & a brother left to look after. Not to mention my precious Kevin and my other munchkin Tonya.

Watch for me, Lo. One of these days God is going to decide it is my time and then we will never be apart again.

I would know how it would be to look into the face of Jesus. One day I will, Praise His Name and thank him for what he has done for me and for all those years he let me have you as a sister! I know that you are happy and that you can breathe well and that those old feet & legs don't hurt anymore.

I wonder how it felt to see Mama & Daddy, Lucille, Grady, Robert, Johnny, Clyde, Lucy, Muriel and Rene & Sis again. Kiss them all for me and tell them I will see them after awhile.

Love you, Sweetheart.

I'll see you later.

~ Peggy

Casseroles

Life is, after all, a casserole. Mama Peggy's casserole recipes are popular for pot-luck food dishes to bring to get-togethers. It's hard to go wrong with a good casserole!

BAKED CORN CASSEROLE

An easy, delicious recipe that you can pretty much just throw together and toss in the oven. What could be easier? And it's yummie. You'll never look at corn the same way again.

Ingredients

- 3 eggs, well beaten
- 2 cans cream style corn
- 1 cup grated cheese
- 1 cup soft bread crumbs
- ¼ cup un-sifted flour
- 1 small onion (or 2 tsp. minced onions)

Instructions

1. Beat the eggs, flour, and onion together.
2. Mix in the corn, cheese, bread crumbs.
3. Pour into a greased 2 quart casserole.
4. Back at 350 degrees for 1 hour.

Recipe type: Casserole
Serves: 8
Prep time: 15 mins
Cook time: 1 hour
Total time: 1 hour 15 mins

Baked Macaroni with Tomato & Cheese

A great baked macaroni recipe with some extra tomato zest. A great, easy casserole for any family meal.

Ingredients

- 1 (7 oz.) pkg. elbow macaroni
- 1 Tbsp. butter
- ¼ c. chopped onion
- 1 can of mushroom soup
- ½ cup milk
- 2 cups shredded cheese
- 1 (16 oz.) can tomatoes, cut up

Instructions

5. Cook macaroni and drain.
6. In medium saucepan, melt butter, add onion, and cook until tender.
7. Add soup and milk.
8. Add cheese and tomatoes.
9. Cook stirring constantly until cheese melts.
10. Combine macaroni with mixture.
11. Pour into 1½ quart casserole dish.
12. Bake at 350 degrees for 30 minutes.

Recipe type: Casserole
Serves: 4
Prep time: 20 mins
Cook time: 30 mins
Total time: 50 mins

BEEF NOODLE CASSEROLE

Ingredients

- 1 ½ lbs. ground beef
- 1 large onion, chopped
- 1 large green pepper, chopped
- ½ cup diced celery
- 1 large can diced tomatoes
- ½ cup tomato paste
- 2 cups Mueller's extra wide noodles
- salt and pepper (to taste)
- 1 ½ cups water
- Medium Cheddar cheese (as much as you want)

Instructions

1. In a large frying pan cook ground beef until it's brown.
2. Drain, but leave 1 ½ Tbsp. of grease.
3. Put onions, bell pepper and celery in grease and sauté until soft.
4. Drain and put all ingredients except noodles in large pot, along with tomatoes and tomato paste!
5. Simmer for about 30 minutes, then add uncooked noodles.
6. Stir well, then cover with lid and turn off burner.
7. After noodles have fluffed up, layer half of mixture in 13 x 9-inch casserole pan.
8. Sprinkle grated cheddar cheese or sliced American cheese over it, and then layer rest of ground beef mixture over that.

9. Top with more grated cheese or sliced cheese.
10. Place in 350 degree oven, just long enough to melt cheese.
11. Enjoy!

Recipe type: Casserole
Serves: 6
Prep time: 15 mins
Cook time: 30 mins
Total time: 45 mins

"This was one of our most requested dishes at Peggy's Restaurant, especially from my Pastor and friend Rev. Eugene Land. He was more like one of us than anyone we knew! What a joy it was to see him come in and make himself at home! I really feel like most of our customers felt the same way, that we were family! We wouldn't have had it any other way! We have such beautiful memories of those years! God Bless all of you, wherever you are!"
~ *Mama Peggy*

Black Eyed Pea Casserole

If you love Southern cooking, you'll love this black eyed pea casserole. And what's not to love? Black eyed peas have always been a staple of any Southern table, and in a casserole they're just delicious!

Ingredients

- 2 Tbsp. butter
- 2 Tbsp. chopped onion
- 1 (3 oz.) jar pimiento, chopped
- 1 can cream of mushroom soup
- 1 cup grated cheddar cheese
- 2 (16 oz.) cans black-eyed peas, drained
- Buttered bread crumbs

Instructions

1. Melt butter in saucepan or skillet; cook onion in butter.
2. Add pimiento, soup, and cheese.
3. Add to peas and pour into greased 2-quart casserole.
4. Top with bread crumbs and bake at 350 degrees for 20 minutes.

Recipe type: Casserole
Serves: 6-8
Prep time: 10 mins
Cook time: 20 mins
Total time: 30 mins

BROCCOLI MAC & CHEESE BAKE

"I love broccoli and I also love macaroni and cheese! This combination makes a killer casserole! I hope you will try it! Enjoy!" ~ *Mama Peggy*

Ingredients

- 3 cups uncooked elbow macaroni
- 4 cups fresh broccoli florets
- ½ cup butter, cubed
- 3 Tbsp. all-purpose flour
- ½ tsp. garlic powder
- ½ tsp. onion powder
- ¼ tsp. pepper
- ⅛ tsp. salt
- 2 cans (12 oz. each) evaporated milk
- 2 ½ cups (10 oz.) cheddar cheese, shredded and divided
- ½ cup crushed Zesta wheat crackers (about 6 crackers)

Instructions

1. Cook macaroni according to pkg. directions, adding broccoli the last 5 minutes-drain.
2. In a large saucepan, melt butter, stir in the flour, garlic powder, onion powder, pepper and salt until smooth; gradually stir in evaporated milk.
3. Bring to a boil.
4. Cook and stir for two minutes or until thickened.
5. Remove from the heat, stir in 2 cups cheese.

6. Place half the macaroni and broccoli in a greased 13 x 9-inch baking dish or pan.
7. Top with half of the cheese sauce.
8. Repeat layers.
9. Sprinkle with crackers crumbs and remaining cheese.
10. Bake, uncovered, at 375 degrees for 20-25 minutes or until bubbly!

Recipe type: Casserole
Serves: 6
Prep time: 15 mins
Cook time: 25 mins
Total time: 40 mins

Chicken Cheese & Rice Casserole

"A yummy twist on a classic dish. The extra cheese brings a hearty richness to this dish. I like to use Chicken Tenders instead of breasts! Your choice!" ~ *Mama Peggy*

Ingredients

- 1 can of Campbell's Condensed Cream of Chicken soup
- 2 cups water
- 1 and ¼ cups uncooked regular, long-grain white rice
- 1 tsp. onion powder
- ¼ tsp. black pepper
- 3 cups frozen mixed vegetables (or carrots and sugar peas)
- 6 skinless, boneless chicken breasts
- ¾ cup shredded cheddar cheese

Instructions

1. Stir soup, water, rice, onion powder, black pepper and vegetables in 3 qt. shallow baking dish.
2. Top with Chicken.
3. Season Chicken with additional black pepper.
4. Cover baking dish.
5. Bake at 375 degrees for 1 hour or when chicken is cooked through and rice is tender!
6. Sprinkle chicken with cheese. Let stand 10 minutes.
7. Stir rice before serving!

Recipe type: Casserole
Serves: 6-8
Prep time: 10 mins
Cook time: 60 mins
Total time: 1 hr 10 mins

CHICKEN AND RICE CASSEROLE

Ingredients

- 2 cups cooked rice
- 2 cups (8 oz.) shredded Monterey Jack cheese
- 1 ½ cups cooked chopped chicken breast meat
- 1 can (12 oz.) canned milk
- ½ cup finely chopped red onion
- 2 large eggs, lightly beaten
- ¼ cup finely chopped cilantro
- 2 Tbsp. butter or margarine, melted 1 Tbsp. diced jalapenos

Instructions

1. Combine rice, cheese, chicken, evaporated milk, onions, eggs, cilantro, butter and jalapenos in prepared casserole dish.
2. Stir well.
3. Bake for 40 to 50 minutes or until knife inserted in center comes out clean.
4. Season with salt.

Recipe type: Casserole
Serves: 8
Prep time: 15 mins
Cook time: 50 mins
Total time: 1 hr 5 mins

CHICKEN SALAD CASSEROLE

Ingredients

- 3 cups chopped cooked chicken
- 1 can cream of chicken soup
- 2 Tbsp. chopped onion
- 2 Tbsp. chopped pimento
- 1 cup chopped celery
- ½ cup chopped almonds
- 1 7 oz. can sliced water chestnuts, drained
- 2 hard-boiled eggs, chopped
- ¾ cup mayonnaise
- 2 cups crushed potato chips

Instructions

1. Combine chicken, soup, onion, pimento, celery, almonds, water chestnuts, eggs and mayonnaise in bowl.
2. Mix well.
3. Spoon into baking dish.
4. Top with potato chips.
5. Bake at 450 degrees until brown. yield: 8 servings.

Recipe type: Casserole
Serves: 8
Prep time: 45 mins
Cook time: 15 mins
Total time: 1 hr

CORNED BEEF CASSEROLE

This is an old-fashioned corned beef casserole that your grandmother might have made.

Ingredients

- 1 8 oz. pkg. shell macaroni
- 1 can Cream of Chicken soup
- 1 12 oz. can of corned beef, cut into small pieces
- 1 cup milk
- ¼ lb. shredded cheese
- 1 small onion (chopped)
- Bread crumbs (buttered)

Instructions

1. Cook your macaroni according to the directions.
2. Drain the macaroni and combine with corned beef, soup, milk, cheese, and onion.
3. Mix your ingredients well and spread into a 9 x 13-inch casserole dish.
4. Top with your buttered breadcrumbs.
5. Bake at 350 degrees for 30 minutes or so.

Recipe type: Casserole
Serves: 6 – 8
Prep time: 15 mins
Cook time: 30 mins
Total time: 45 min

CREAMY CHICKEN AND RICE BAKE

Ingredients

- 1 can (12 oz.) evaporated milk
- 1 pkg. (3 oz.) cream cheese, softened
- 1 can of cream of chicken soup
- ½ cup water
- ½ tsp. garlic powder
- ⅛ tsp. ground pepper
- 1 bag (16 oz.) frozen broccoli, cauliflower, and carrot mix, thawed
- 2 cups cubed, precooked chicken
- 1 ½ cups uncooked instant white rice
- ½ cup (2 oz.) shredded mild cheddar cheese

Instructions

1. Preheat oven to 350 degrees.
2. Grease 13 x 9-inch baking pan.
3. Combine milk and cream cheese with wire whisk until smooth.
4. Add soup, water, garlic powder and black pepper; mix well.
5. Add vegetables, chicken and rice.
6. Cover tightly with foil.

7. Bake for 35 minutes.
8. Remove cover and top with cheese.
9. Continue baking uncovered for 10 to 15 minutes until cheese is melted and mixture is bubbly, let stand 5 minutes before serving.

Recipe type: Casserole
Serves: 8
Prep time: 15 mins
Cook time: 50 mins
Total time: 1 hr 5 mins

CROCKPOT CHICKEN AND RICE CASSEROLE

Ingredients

- 4 chicken breasts
- 1 can cream of celery soup
- 1 can cream of chicken soup
- 1 can cream of mushroom soup
- 2 stalks celery, diced
- 1 large onion, chopped
- ½ tsp. poultry seasoning
- 3 cloves garlic, minced
- 1 cup Minute Rice

Instructions

1. Mix the cans of soup with the rice at the bottom of the crock pot. You may substitute the type of soup you use in any combination (for example: 2 cans cream of chicken soup and 1 can celery soup.)

2. Add the diced celery, onion, and garlic and stir.
3. Submerge the chicken in the soup.
4. Turn heat to high for 10 minutes, then reduce to medium and cook for 4-5 hours. Or cook on high for 3-4 hours.

Recipe type: Casserole
Serves: 6
Prep time: 15 mins
Cook time: 4-5 hrs
Total time: 4-5 hrs 15 mins

Easy Chicken & Biscuits

Ingredients

- 1 can Campbell's condensed Cream of Celery Soup
- 1 can Campbell's condensed Cream of Potato Soup
- ⅔ cup milk
- ½ tsp. poultry seasoning
- ⅛ tsp. black pepper
- 2 cups frozen mixed vegetables
- 2 cups cubed cooked chicken (or turkey)
- 1 pkg. refrigerated biscuits (7.5 oz.)

Instructions

1. Stir soups, milk, poultry seasoning, black pepper, vegetables, and chicken in 2qt. shallow baking dish.
2. Bake at 400 degrees 20 minutes or until chicken mixture is hot and bubbling.

3. Stir chicken mixture.
4. Top with biscuits.
5. Bake 15 minutes or until biscuits are golden brown.

Recipe type: Casserole
Serves: 8
Prep time: 10 mins
Cook time: 35 mins
Total time: 45 mins

Easy Chicken Pot Pie

Ingredients

- 1 can Campbell's Cream of Potato soup
- ¾ cup milk
- ⅛ tsp. ground black pepper
- 1 cup frozen mixed vegetables
- 2 cans (4.5 oz. each) Swanson Premium Chunk Chicken Breast, drained
- 1 egg
- 1 cup all-purpose baking Mix

Instructions

1. Preheat oven to 400 degrees.
2. Mix soup, ¼ cup milk, pepper, vegetables and chicken in 9-inch. pie pan.
3. Mix remaining milk, egg and baking mix.
4. Pour over chicken mixture.
5. Bake 30 minutes or until hot and topping is golden.

Recipe type: Casserole
Serves: 8
Prep time: 10 mins
Cook time: 30 mins
Total time: 40 mins

GROUND BEEF AND POTATO CASSEROLE

"I developed this recipe for Peggy's Restaurant one day and it caught on pretty quickly! My sister Sherry just loved it and begged me to make it again. I hope you try it. Enjoy!" ~ *Mama Peggy*

Ingredients

- 2 lbs. Ground Beef
- 1 Tbsp. shortening
- 1 medium onion, chopped
- ½ tsp salt
- ¼ tsp. pepper
- 1 can cream of mushroom soup
- 6 or 8 medium potatoes, sliced
- 2 cups cheddar cheese, grated

Instructions

1. Preheat Brown ground beef in shortening in skillet, stirring until crumbly; drain.
2. Put onions in skillet with the same grease from hamburger!
3. Cook until soft, then drain.
4. Mix with ground beef.

5. Mix soup and a small amount of boiling water in bowl.
6. Layer potatoes, ground beef mixture and soup mixture one half at a time.
7. Sprinkle half of cheese over all, then layer other half and sprinkle with rest of cheese.
8. Bake at 350 degrees for 1 hour. May add more water for desired consistency!

Recipe type: Casserole
Serves: 8
Prep time: 20 mins
Cook time: 60 mins
Total time: 1 hr 20 mins

HOMESTYLE GREEN BEAN CASSEROLE

"Green Bean Casserole has also been a staple on the Thanksgiving table for a lot of years! Well! This is a newer version! It will be on my Thanksgiving table! I hope you try it!" ~ *Mama Peggy*

Ingredients

- 1 ½ lb. fresh green beans, trimmed
- 2 Tbsp. butter
- ¼ all-purpose flour
- 1 ½ cups 2% milk
- ½ cup fat free buttermilk
- 1 Tbsp. Ranch dressing mix
- 2 tsp. thyme (fresh) chopped
- ¼ tsp. salt
- ¼ tsp. pepper
- 1 tsp. butter
- 1 (8 oz.) pkg. sliced mushrooms
- Vegetable cooking spray
- 1 cup French fried onions (crushed)
- ½ cup panko (Japanese breadcrumbs)
- 2 plum tomatoes, seeded and chopped

Instructions

1. Preheat oven to 350 degrees.
2. Cook green beans in boiling water until they are done; drain.
3. Plunge into ice water to stop the cooking process; Drain and pat dry.

4. Melt 2 Tbsp. butter in large pot.
5. Whisk in flour until smooth.
6. Cook, whisking constantly, 1 minute.
7. Gradually whisk in 1½ cups milk; whisking constantly 3-4 minutes or until sauce is thickened and bubbly.
8. Remove from heat and whisk in buttermilk and next four ingredients.
9. Melt 1 tsp. butter in a medium skillet over med. high heat; add mushrooms and sauté 6 to 8 minutes or until lightly browned.
10. Remove from heat; let stand 5 minutes.
11. Gently toss mushrooms and green beans in buttermilk sauce.
12. Place in a 13 x 9-inch or 3-quart baking dish coated with cooking spray.
13. Combine French fried onions and the next two ingredients; sprinkle over green bean mixture.
14. Bake at 350 degrees for 25 to 30 minutes or until golden brown!

Recipe type: Casserole
Serves: 8
Prep time: 30 mins
Cook time: 30 mins
Total time: 1 hr

KING RANCH CHICKEN CASSEROLE

Ingredients

- 4 large chicken breasts
- 2 celery ribs, cut into 3 pieces each
- 2 carrots
- 3 tsp. salt
- 2 Tbsp. butter
- 1 medium onion, chopped
- 1 medium-size bell pepper, chopped
- 1 garlic, pressed
- 1 (10 ¾ oz.) can cream of mushroom soup
- 1 can cream of chicken soup
- 2 (10 cans diced tomatoes and green chilies, drained
- 1 tsp. dried oregano
- 1 tsp. ground cumin
- 1 tsp. Mexican-style chili powder *
- 3 cups grated Cheddar cheese
- 12 (6-inch) fajita-size corn tortillas, cut into ½-inch strips

Instructions

1. Place chicken, celery, carrots and salt in a large pot or Dutch oven with water to cover.
2. Bring to a boil over medium heat; reduce heat to low.
3. Cover and simmer 50 minutes to 1 hour or until chicken is done. Remove from heat.
4. Remove chicken from broth: cool 30 minutes.

5. Remove and reserve ¾ cooking liquid.
6. Strain any remaining cooking liquid and reserve for another use.
7. Preheat oven to 350 degrees.
8. Melt butter in a large skillet over medium to high heat.
9. Add onion and sauté 6 to 7 minutes or until tender.
10. Add bell pepper and garlic and sauté 3 to 4 minutes.
11. Stir in reserved 3/4 cup cooking liquid, cream of mushroom soup and next 5 ingredients, stirring occasionally, 8 minutes.
12. Skin and bone chicken; shred meat into bite size pieces.
13. Layer half of chicken in a lightly greased 13 x 9-inch baking pan.
14. Top with soup mixture and 1 cup Cheddar cheese.
15. Cover with half of corn tortilla strips.
16. Repeat layers once.
17. Top with remaining 1 cup cheese.
18. Bake at 350° for 55 minutes to 1 hour or until bubbly.
19. Let stand 10 minutes before serving.

* 1 tsp. chili powder and ⅛ tsp. ground red pepper may be substituted for Mexican style chili powder.

Recipe type: Casserole
Serves: 8
Prep time: 38 mins
Cook time: 116 mins
Total time: 1 hr 56 mins

MEXICAN CHICKEN CASSEROLE

Ingredients

- 4 large chicken breasts
- ¼ tsp. garlic powder
- 1 can Rotel tomatoes and chilies
- 1 can cream of chicken soup
- 1 soup can of evaporated canned milk
- tortilla chips
- Grated cheddar cheese (about two cups – or more if you prefer).

Instructions

1. Boil chicken breasts until done.
2. Drain and shred chicken. Set aside.
3. Combine tomatoes and chilies in large bowl, with chicken soup, soup can of evaporated milk, ¼ tsp. garlic powder.
4. Add chicken.
5. Stir together.
6. Spray 12 x 9-inch baking pan or dish with Pam.
7. Crush tortilla chips and place in bottom of pan.
8. Pour meat mixture over top of crushed chips.
9. Sprinkle grated cheddar cheese over all.
10. Bake at 350 degrees until bubbly and lightly browned.

Recipe type: Casserole
Serves: 6
Prep time: 15 mins
Cook time: 40 mins
Total time: 55 mins

PEGGY'S BROCCOLI CASSEROLE

"This was another favorite at Peggy's Restaurant. Try it! You'll like it. I guarantee it!!!" ~ *Mama Peggy*

Ingredients

- 2 pkg. frozen broccoli
- 1 onion, diced
- ½ stick margarine (or butter)
- 1 cup mayonnaise
- 2 eggs, beaten
- 1 can cream of mushroom soup (or cream of chicken, if you prefer)
- 2 cups grated cheddar cheese
- 2 cups cracker crumbs

Instructions

1. Cook broccoli and drain it.
2. Sauté onion in the ½ stick of margarine until soft.
3. Mix all ingredients except the cheese and cracker crumbs.
4. Sprinkle cheese over casserole and then sprinkle cracker crumbs.
5. Bake uncovered at 350 degrees for 45 minutes.

6. You can make ahead of time and refrigerate or freeze!

Recipe type: Casserole
Serves: 6
Prep time: 25 mins
Cook time: 45 mins
Total time: 1 hr 10 mins

PEGGY'S PINTO BEAN CASSEROLE

"I've used Blackeyed peas instead of pintos. Loved it! I've also replaced cream of chicken soup with Cream of Mushroom soup! Very good!" ~ *Mama Peggy*

Ingredients

- 1 lb. hamburger meat
- 1 large onion, chopped
- 1 large green pepper, chopped
- 2 cans pinto beans, drained
- 1 lg. can of diced tomatoes, with juice
- 1 can of Ro-tel mild diced tomatoes and green chilis
- 1 can of cream of chicken soup

Instructions

1. Brown ground beef, onions and bell pepper in large saucepan, drain.
2. Combine with other ingredients, mixing well!
3. Spray 15 x 9-inch pan with cooking spray.

4. Pour all in baking pan.
5. Prepare topping:

    - 1 cup self-rising flour
    - 1 cup self-rising corn meal
    - 2 eggs
    - 1 Tbsp. mayonnaise
    - 2 cups grated cheddar cheese

    Beat first four ingredients together, then stir in cheese!

6. Pour topping slowly over the pinto bean mixture.
7. Place in 400-degree oven.
8. Bake for 30 or 40 minutes! Just until real brown on top!

Recipe type: Casserole
Serves: 6
Prep time: 15 mins
Cook time: 40 mins
Total time: 55 mins

Pork Chop Potato Bake Casserole

Ingredients

- 6 Pork chops
- 1 can Cream of celery, or mushroom soup
- ½ cup milk
- ½ cup sour cream
- Salt and pepper
- 24 oz. O'Brien potatoes or hash browns
- 1 cup shredded Cheddar cheese
- 1 can Durkee onions

Instructions

1. Brown pork chops in a small amount of oil.
2. Sprinkle in salt and pepper.
3. In a large bowl, combine potatoes, soup, milk, sour cream, half the shredded cheese, and half of the fried onions.
4. Spoon into 13 x 9-inch baking dish.
5. Arrange pork chops on top and cover.
6. Bake at 350 degrees for 40 minutes.
7. Top with remaining cheese and onions and bake 5 minutes longer, uncovered.

Recipe type: Casserole
Serves: 4
Prep time: 20 mins
Cook time: 40 mins
Total time: 1 hr

Sweet Potato Casserole

No recipe collection is complete without sweet potato casserole. But the debate continues. Is it a side dish? Is it a casserole? Is it a dessert? You should make some and help us figure this out!

Ingredients

- 4 cups sweet potatoes
- 1½ sticks butter
- 2 eggs
- 1 cup sugar
- 1 tsp. vanilla flavoring
- 1 cup brown sugar
- ⅓ cup flour
- ⅓ cup butter, melted
- 1 cup chopped pecans

Instructions

1. Mix the sweet potatoes, butter sticks, eggs, sugar, and vanilla together in a casserole dish.
2. Mix the remaining ingredients together in a bowl and spread over top.
3. Back at 375 degrees for 30 minutes.

Recipe type: Casserole
Serves: 10 – 12
Prep time: 15 mins
Cook time: 30 mins
Total time: 45 mins

Squash Casserole

"This is a new twist on a squash casserole that I think you will like! Nearly every squash casserole is basically the same! I love it myself and I will always be searching for new ways to prepare the dishes that you and I enjoy! I think this one is a winner!" ~ *Mama Peggy*

Ingredients

- 4 lb. yellow squash, sliced
- 1 large sweet onion, finely chopped
- 1 cup (4 oz.) freshly shredded cheddar cheese
- 1 cup mayonnaise
- 2 Tbsp. chopped basil
- 1 tsp. garlic salt
- 1 tsp. black pepper
- 2 large eggs, lightly beaten
- 2 cups soft breadcrumbs, divided
- 1 ¼ cups (5 oz.) shredded Parmesan cheese
- 2 Tbsp. butter, melted
- ½ cup crushed French fried onions

Instructions

1. Preheat oven to 350 degrees.
2. Cook yellow squash and onion in boiling water to cover in a large pot 8 minutes or just until the vegetables are tender; drain squash mixture well.
3. Combine squash mixture, shredded Cheddar cheese, next 5 ingredients, 1 cup bread crumbs and ¾ cup Parmesan cheese.

4. Spoon into a lightly greased 13 x 9-inch baking dish.
   5. Stir together melted butter, French fried onions, and remaining 1 cup the breadcrumbs and ½ cup of Parmesan cheese.
   6. Sprinkle over squash mixture.
   7. Bake at 350 degrees for 35 to 40 minutes or until set. ENJOY!

Recipe type: Casserole
Serves: 6
Prep time: 20 mins
Cook time: 40 mins
Total time: 1 hr

THAT'S NA-CHO CASSEROLE!

Ingredients

- 1 to 1½ lbs. lean ground beef
- 1 large can refried beans
- 1 package of taco seasoning
- 1 can Ro-Tel tomatoes with chiles (mild)
- 1 small container cottage cheese
- 1 medium bag shredded sharp cheddar cheese
- 1 large bag of tortilla chips
- Salsa

Instructions

1. Brown the beef, drained the grease.
2. Add taco seasoning and water as directed on taco package.

3. Mix in refried beans and the Ro-Tel tomatoes.
4. Set this mixture aside.
5. In a large baking dish (I use the aluminum kind because they are bigger and deeper) and spray with pam or some non-stick spray.
6. Put a layer of chips along the bottom of the pan.
7. Then put a layer of the beef/bean mixture.
8. Add about ⅓ of the cottage cheese.
9. Then add about ¼ of the package of cheese (we like a LOT of cheese so I usually buy extra).
10. Next add about 5-6 Tbsp. of salsa.
11. This is your first layer. Repeat this process and end with a layer of cheese.
12. Bake in a pre-heated 350 degree oven until cheese is melted and sides are bubbling.
13. Serve hot and top with the cold fresh garnishes.

Garnish: Fresh chopped onions, green peppers, tomatoes, lettuces, black olives, and I usually get a jar of jalapenos because the fresh ones burn me up! Sour Cream. Shredded cheddar cheese. Salsa.

Recipe Shared by Victoria Sadler Lovelace[1]
Recipe type: Main Dish
Serves: 10
Prep time: 15 mins
Cook time: 20 mins
Total time: 35 mins

---

[1] Sadler Family Recipes

Vegetable Casserole

"Delicious casserole! I believe it will be one of your favorites!" ~ *Mama Peggy*

Ingredients

- 1 can white shoe peg corn, drained
- 1 French style green beans, drained
- 1 can cream of celery soup
- 1 cup sharp cheese (grated)
- 1 cup celery, chopped
- 1 green pepper, chopped
- 1 cup onion, chopped
- 1 (8 oz.) container sour cream
- Salt and Pepper to taste

Instructions

1. Preheat oven to 350 degrees.
2. Mix all together and place in 9 x 13-inch pan.
3. Combine ½ box cheese crackers, crumbled, ½ stick margarine, melted, and 1 pkg. slivered almonds.
4. Pour on top of casserole mixture and bake for 1 hour!

Recipe type: Casserole
Serves: 6
Prep time: 10 mins
Cook time: 60 mins
Total time: 1 hr 10 mins

Vidalia Onion Casserole

Ingredients

- ½ cup butter
- 4 Vidalias sliced in ¼-inch rings
- 15 Saltine crackers (crushed)
- 1 can mushroom soup
- 2 eggs (beaten)
- ½ to ¾ cup milk
- 1 cup shredded cheddar cheese

Instructions

1. Melt butter in pan over medium heat and cook onions until clear.
2. Reserve 3 Tbsp. of crumbs for topping and place remaining crumbs in the bottom of greased 2 qt. casserole dish.
3. Remove onions from pan with slotted spoon.
4. Add soup and onions in alternate layers until full.
5. Combine eggs and butter, pour over onions.
6. Top with cheese and remaining crumbs.
7. Bake at 350 degrees for 20 to 30 minutes or until brown and bubbly.

Recipe type: Casserole
Serves: 4-6
Prep time: 15 mins
Cook time: 30 mins
Total time: 45 mins

Peggy's Blog – In Church Again
January 28, 2008

It felt so good to be in church again. Everyone seemed genuinely glad to see me. Preacher Land is still recuperating at home. He came back to the pulpit too soon and had a relapse. He has always been a "Go getter" (another Southern saying). I can honestly say that I have sat in a pew for a long time and I have never been bored at all when listening to him preach or teach. Our prayers are that God will touch him and heal him so that he can be about his Father's business, doing the one thing he loves doing and that is preaching the gospel.

I am a little tired tonight but so glad to be back in the choir. I love to sing but I had a little trouble this morning. I worried about it all afternoon and finally went into my bedroom, and got down on my knees before God. I told Him that I was sorry for the time I have wasted when I could have been in church this past year. I asked His forgiveness and told Him just how I felt about singing. That I didn't have too many more years on earth, but what time I had left I wanted to praise Him through Singing and if He wanted me to sit with the congregation I would, but if He wanted me to sing, then He was going to have to help my voice, and I was just going to leave it at His feet. I went on to choir practice at 5 p.m. We practiced some on our Easter music and the two songs we were to do for the service. When we sang our first song, I just breezed through it, no problems.

Then when we sang our next song I did even better and cold chills ran all over me. When we went down to sit in the sanctuary, the lady behind me leaned forward and patted me on the back and said "I'm so glad you're back in the choir".

I don't know about you but I think God gave me my answer!

Gravy

Chicken Gravy

This is a simple chicken gravy recipe which goes great over dressing, turkey or chicken.

Ingredients

- 1 can cream of chicken soup
- 2 cups of chicken broth
- 3 hard-boiled eggs

Instructions

1. Mix soup and chicken broth with a wire whisk in a medium pot.
2. Put on burner and allow to get hot.
3. Check to see if salt and pepper is needed.
4. Add sliced boiled eggs.
5. Also, pieces of chicken will make it taste even better.
6. If you want thinner dressing, use two pans!

Recipe type: Gravy
Serves: 10
Prep time: 15 mins
Cook time: 15 mins
Total time: 30 mins

Chocolate Gravy

Chocolate gravy was a treat in the Chaney household when Mama Peggy was growing up. It seems to be unique to the Appalachians, but made it at least as far as the North Carolina foothills.

Ingredients

- ¼ cup unsweetened cocoa powder
- 3 Tbsp. all-purpose flour
- 1 cup sugar
- 1 cup milk
- 1 tsp. pure vanilla extract
- 1 Tbsp. butter

Instructions

1. Combine cocoa, flour and sugar in a heavy saucepan.
2. Whisk in milk.
3. Heat over medium heat until mixture comes to a boil and thickens (about 5 minutes).
4. Add vanilla and butter to hot mixture.
5. Serve warm over biscuits.

Recipe type: Gravy
Serves: 4
Prep time: 10 mins
Cook time: 5 mins
Total time: 15 mins

PEGGY'S BREAKFAST GRAVY

This is Mama Peggy's gravy recipe as served up at Peggy's Restaurant in Kings Mountain, North Carolina for almost 30 years. We always eat it by crumbling up some fresh made biscuits and covering them with some warm gravy. But people also ate it with spoon from a plate, and biscuits or loaf bread on the side. Throw in a few pieces of bacon or sausage, and you have a well-rounded Southern breakfast.

Ingredients

- 8-12 slices bacon
- 3 Tbsp. flour
- 2 cups milk
- 1 cup evaporated (canned) milk
- 1 Tbsp. pepper
- 2 Tbsp. butter (just in case)

Instructions

1. Over medium-high heat, cook bacon in a skillet until crisp.
2. Remove bacon and set aside (you can eat it if you like). Leave all the fat and yummy bits in the pan.
3. Turn down the heat to medium.
4. Add 3 Tbsp. of flour and begin to whisk.
5. If flour starts balling up, you don't have enough fat. Bring out the butter! But add only if you need it.
6. Keep whisking the flour until the mixture turns light brown.

7. Add your milk while stirring. First the milk, then the evaporated milk.
8. Once the milk is in, it's just lots of whisking and waiting. Make sure not to walk away during this part. You need to stick with it, whisking and scraping down the sides. After a few minutes, it will thicken up.
9. Once the gravy has thickened, add ground black pepper to taste.
10. Salt to taste.
11. Continue whisking until the gravy is as thick as you like.
12. Serve on a plate, in a bowl or (best of all) over fresh baked biscuits.

Recipe type: Gravy
Serves: 6
Prep time: 5 mins
Cook time: 10 mins
Total time: 15 mins

Peggy's Blog – You Can't Go Home Again!
November 3, 2008

You Can't go Home Again!

All my life I have heard this phrase and I thought of it once again as I drove past our old house on Crescent Hill this morning. It looked so forlorn and sad! My heart was heavy as I looked at it and remembered all the happy days Kevin, Loretta and I spent there. The endless hours I spent in the yard. Hauling rocks from Martin Marietta to build flower beds. The day lilies I carried from my Mama's yard when I was married and carried from place to place as I moved through the years.

At one time I had around sixty rose bushes, not counting all the different other plants scattered here and there around the yards. Front and back! I would come home from the restaurant, rest a few hours and then outside I would go, happy as a lark, working with my flowers. Sometimes it would be dark before I decided to come in, reluctantly.

One day, on my birthday, Ted Ford asked Loretta what she thought I would like for my birthday. She told him, jokingly, that I would probably kill for a fish pond. Well, what do you know! He sent one of his employees to our house and I got my fish pond. I used to sit for hours by that pond, listening to the water and watching those fish swim happily along. Cares and worries seemed so far removed at those times.

The grass is overgrown there now. I try to peek at the back yard as I pass by but the weeds are so high. I could see that my yellow climbing rose was in bloom though. I remembered walking around in that back yard, all of our cats following behind my heels. Especially "Stripe". If I walked across the street to the neighbor's house, I would look down and there she would be. There was a bird who nested in our yard every year and she hated Stripe for some reason. Every time she went out into the yard, that bird would swoop down and peck her in the head or else try with all her might to. Stripe would mosey along just like she didn't know that bird was even there. I would laugh and laugh at their antics.

If I close my eyes, I can see Kevin sitting in that swing I had bought him, both arms on the back of it, just swinging and dreaming about a better tomorrow. I can also remember the day he was working in the yard! He had let his hair grow out and this day it got too much for him. He came in the house and much to my shock and horror, went into the bathroom and started shaving his head. He cut it with sheer abandon, didn't matter which way that shaver was going, but as it worked out, he did a good job (for his first time). haha

I could probably sit here for hours remembering and reflecting but as I turned the corner to go to my sister Sue's house, there at the corner of the front yard of our old house sat that big maple tree that Kevin and I had so long ago planted, and it was ablaze with the most gorgeous yellow, gold foliage. It almost took my breath away.

At that moment I knew that one day, some family would move into that old house, probably with the same hopes and dreams that Kevin, Lo and I had. They would have a chance to make all their dreams come true and our old house would be a happy place again. Just as it was with the three of us. God Bless Them.

Appetizers

ANN'S OVEN-ROASTED POTATOES

Ingredients

- 1 envelope Lipton Savory Herb with Garlic soup mix
- 2 lbs. potatoes, washed & cut into chunks (with skins)
- ⅓ cup olive oil

Instructions

1. Preheat oven at 450 degrees.
2. Mix soup mix and oil in large bowl, add potatoes & toss until coated.
3. Place potatoes evenly in baking pan and bake at 450 degrees for 40 minutes, turning every ten minutes.

"If you want onions… after putting potatoes in oven, chop 1 or 2 onions in same bowl. Scrape sides of bowl for what little soup/oil mix left to coat onions a little. I add a little garlic powder. When turning potatoes 2nd time, fold in onions, baking them the additional 20 minutes (turning all again after 10 minutes).

"When Ann (my niece) brought these to a family dinner at Church, she said she used 4 lbs. of potatoes & 2 large onions. She also put strips of bell pepper and banana peppers from her garden, when she added the onions!

"I fixed these for supper last week for Sherry and me! They were so good with Pinto beans and homemade biscuits.

We ate too much because they were absolutely, unbelievably delicious! Then I warmed the leftovers for the next meal! Man! You gotta try them! ENJOY!!!!!"

~ Mama Peggy

Recipe type: Appetizer
Serves: 6
Prep time: 20 mins
Cook time: 40 mins
Total time: 1 hr

CHEESE BALL 1

Ingredients

- 3 (8 oz.) cream cheese (room temperature)
- 4 small jars dried beef
- 1 small onion, chopped fine
- 2 Tbsp. Accent flavor enhancer
- 3 Tbsp. Worcestershire sauce

Instructions

1. Chop very fine 3 small jars dried beef.
2. Combine onion with cream cheese, Accent, and Worcestershire sauce.
3. Work this really good together and form into 2 balls.
4. Take fourth jar of dried beef and wrap both cheese balls really good.
5. Refrigerate several hours to marinate. (These will freeze well.)

Recipe type: Appetizer
Serves: 30
Prep time: 20 mins
Cook time: 0 mins
Total time: 20 mins

CHEESE BALL 2

Ingredients

- 2 (8 oz.) pkg. cream cheese
- 1 small can crushed pineapple (drained)
- 2 cups chopped nuts
- ¼ cup green pepper
- ¼ tsp. salt
- 2 Tbsp. onion

Instructions

1. Add pineapple to cheese; mix pepper, onion, and salt into mixture.
2. Add ½ cup nuts.
3. Form into 2 large balls.
4. Cover with remaining nuts and refrigerate.

Recipe type: Appetizer
Serves: 30
Prep time: 20 mins
Cook time: 0 mins
Total time: 20 mins

CHEESY SPINACH AND BACON DIP

Ingredients

- 1 lb. Velveeta Cheese
- 1 pkg. (10 oz.) frozen spinach
- 4 oz. (half of 8 oz. pkg.) cream cheese
- 1 can (10 ½ oz.) Ro-Tel diced tomatoes & green chilies
- 8 slices bacon

Instructions

1. Cut Velveeta Cheese into ½-inch cubes.
2. Place in large microwaveable bowl.
3. Add frozen spinach (thawed and drained), cream cheese (cut up), Ro-Tel diced tomatoes & green chilies (undrained), bacon (cooked crisp, drained and crumbly).
4. Microwave on high 5 minutes or until Velveeta is completely melted and the mixture is well blended (stirring after 3 minutes or so).
5. Serve hot with tortilla chips or cut-up vegetables.
6. Makes 4 cups or about 32 servings of 2 Tbsp. each.

Recipe type: Appetizer
Serves: 32
Prep time: 10 mins
Cook time: 20 mins
Total time: 30 mins

CHOCOLATE CHIP CHEESE BALL

Ingredients

- 1 pkg. cream cheese (8 oz), softened
- ½ cup Butter -softened
- ¼ tsp. vanilla extract
- ¾ cup confectioner's sugar
- 2 Tbsp. Brown sugar
- ¾ cup miniature semi-sweet chocolate chips
- ¾ cup finely chopped pecans
- Graham crackers

Instructions

1. In a mixing bowl, mix the cream cheese, butter and vanilla until fluffy.
2. Gradually add sugars, and beat just until combined.
3. Stir in chocolate chips.
4. Cover and refrigerate for 2 hours.
5. Place cream cheese mixture on a large piece of plastic wrap, shape into a ball.
6. Refrigerate 1 hour.
7. Just before serving roll cheese ball in pecans.
8. Serve with graham crackers.

Recipe type: Appetizer
Serves: 30
Prep time: 20 mins
Cook time: 3 hrs
Total time: 3 hrs 20 mins

CRAB DIP

Ingredients

- 1 ctn. sour cream
- 1 can crab meat
- 1 pkg. dried onion soup mix

Instructions

1. Mix well and serve.

Recipe type: Appetizer
Serves: 20
Prep time: 10 mins
Cook time: 0 hrs
Total time: 10 mins

DEVILED CHEESE PUFFS

Ingredients

- ½ cup margarine (or butter)
- 1 cup boiling water
- 1 cup flour
- 1 tsp. salt
- 4 eggs

Instructions

1. Mix butter in water.
2. Add flour and salt all at once and stir well.

3. Cook until ball forms and does not separate.
4. Remove from heat.
5. Add eggs, one at a time, beating after each until smooth.
6. Drop by teaspoons, 1 inch apart, on greased baking sheet.
7. Bake at 450 degrees for 25 minutes.
8. Cool on rack.
9. When cool, cut off top and fill with deviled cheese filling (listed below).

Deviled Cheese

Ingredients

- 2 cups grated cheese
- 1 tsp. Worcestershire sauce
- 6 Tbsp. mayonnaise
- ½ tsp. mustard
- 2 tsp. onion, grated
- 8 drops of Tabasco
- ½ celery seed
- 2 tsp. horseradish

Instructions

1. Mix ingredients.
2. Fill puffs.
3. Refrigerate until ready to use.
4. Heat at 300 degrees until cheese melts and is heated thoroughly.

"This filling also makes great grilled cheese sandwiches."
~ *Mama Peggy*

Recipe type: Appetizer
Serves: 16
Prep time: 30 mins
Cook time: 25 mins
Total time: 55 mins

OLIVE CHEESE BALL

Ingredients

- 2 (8 oz.) pkg. cream cheese
- 1 lb. mild or medium cheddar cheese (grated)
- ½ or 1 pkg. Italian dressing mix
- ¼ cup olives (chopped)
- 2 tsp. olive juice
- 1 cup pecans (chopped)

Instructions

1. Mix well with hands and roll in pecans. Delicious!

"The best Cheese Ball ever!!!" ~ *Mama Peggy*

Recipe type: Appetizer
Serves: 30
Prep time: 10 mins
Cook time: 0 mins
Total time: 10 mins

Peggy's Restaurant Livermush Biscuit

One of the great mysteries around Kings Mountain, North Carolina back in the Peggy's Restaurant days was always why the livermush biscuits at Peggy's tasted so much better than anywhere else. The answer might surprise you. Here's how you can make your own.

Ingredients

- 1 1-lb. block of livermush (we used Mack's at Peggy's)
- 8 biscuits

Instructions

1. Prepare your biscuits (use Peggy's Southern Style Buttermilk Biscuits recipe, or Mary B's frozen buttermilk biscuits).
2. Slice livermush into 8-10 pieces.
3. Deep fry livermush in a deep fryer (such as a FryDaddy) until pieces begin to float.
4. Remove livermush and drain off oil, pat dry with a paper towel.
5. Serve each piece on a sliced biscuit with mayonnaise on the bottom (it's only authentic with Duke's) and yellow mustard on the top.
6. Now you've made yourself a Peggy's Restaurant livermush biscuit!

Recipe type: Appetizer
Serves: 8
Prep time: 20 mins
Cook time: 20 mins
Total time: 40 mins

So... what *is* livermush?

It's quite possible some of you don't even know what livermush is. Livermush is a Southern food product composed of pig liver, head parts, and cornmeal, most commonly spiced with pepper and sage. In our neck of the woods in the foothills of North Carolina (or more specifically in Kings Mountain, where Mama Peggy was from and Peggy's Restaurant operated), livermush was thought as a Southern delicacy.

Livermush originates in the Carolinas. Shelby, North Carolina, the city just west of Kings Mountain, hosts an annual Livermush Exposition and is home to two of best known brands of livermush, Mack's (which was used at Peggy's Restaurant) and Jenkins. Other North Carolina cities which host livermush festivals are Drexel and Marion.

Livermush is typically pan fried, but at Peggy's Restaurant it was deep fried in what we called the fry-o-later. Deep frying gives the livermush the delicious outer crust that most folks who has them associated with a Peggy's Restaurant livermush biscuit. You don't have to eat livermush on a biscuit, though. It's just at home taking the place of bacon or sausage on a Southern breakfast plate of eggs and grits.

Just for the record, the only people who think livermush is "similar to scrapple" are our Northern friends. It's similar in concept, maybe, but very different in result. Most Southerners won't touch scrapple, no way, no how.

SAUSAGE DIP

Ingredients

- 1 lb. Neese's Sausage (mild or hot)
- 1 6 oz. pkg. cream cheese
- 1 can Rotel diced tomatoes and green chives.

Instructions

1. Cook sausage in frying pan until well done.
2. Place sausage in crock pot, and thoroughly mix in other ingredients.
3. Keep warm on lowest heat.
4. Serve with tortillas or choice of chips.

"This is yummy!" ~ *Mama Peggy*

Recipe type: Appetizer
Serves: 20
Prep time: 10 mins
Cook time: 10 mins
Total time: 20 mins

SPINACH BALLS

Ingredients

- 4 large eggs
- 2 (10 oz.) pkg. frozen Spinach
- 1 cup finely chopped minced onion
- ¾ cup Parmesan cheese grated
- ¾ cup melted margarine
- ½ tsp. garlic salt
- 2 ½ cups seasoned stuffing mix

Instructions

1. Cook spinach according to package directions.
2. Drain and squeeze dry.
3. Stir in onion, cheese, butter and salt.
4. When thoroughly blended, stir in stuffing mix.
5. Shape into balls using about a teaspoonful of mixture.
6. Place on cookie sheet and bake at 350 degrees for about 12 minutes or until golden brown.
7. Makes 6 dozen.

Recipe type: Appetizer
Serves: 36
Prep time: 12 mins
Cook time: 10 mins
Total time: 32 mins

Peggy's Blog – A Drastic Decision
December 17, 2008

A few weeks ago, I made a drastic decision. I decided to go gray! After all these years, I finally got tired of the hair color, and everything that goes with it. So, before I could change my mind, I dug a gray wig out that I had bought about a year ago, combed and styled it, threw it on my head and waited for the fun to begin. I walked in to my sister Sherry's apartment. Her faced dropped and she said right off the bat "I don't like that gray hair". I said right back "Get used to it". This is the new ME!

Well, I have to admit it took some getting used too. But I'm slowly, surely getting used to it, and I've almost quit jumping every time I pass a mirror and wondering who that old lady is following me around. I get a kick out of walking in someplace, where most people there know me, and see the startled looks on their faces when they realize it's me.

But there are some real advantages to gray hair. For one thing, people seem to go out of their way to be nice to older, white haired ladies. Yesterday, my sister Sue and I were in Gastonia, N.C. visiting our older sister, who, by the way, will be ninety-one years old on January 12th, 2009. She is in a nursing home and has been for a good many years. Sue can't walk too good because of a bad hip that she broke 7 years ago. When we walk across the street I always hold her hand and cars will stop for us and people, male and female, will smile and wave at us.

I have found that, around our part of the country, most people are really decent, hard-working people (who love their older parents), and it shows in their kindness to seniors.

Even our waiter sort of hovered over us, even telling us that he WAS going to take very good care of us. He did, too! Of course, when we left I had to almost drag Sue out of the restaurant because she wants to talk to everyone who looks her way. God forbid that they smile at her too! Her daughter Debbie tells us that we could talk to trees.

My heart is so full of love for my sister Sue. She is a little opinionated and will argue a little if she THINKS she is right and will argue a lot if she KNOWS she is right, but she loves her sister Peggy with a passion and leaves no doubt in my mind that she would lay down her life for me. As I would for her. A lady that would get up at 7 a.m. to feed five stray cats that she took in, not counting about 3 or more that come to her door every morning hunting food, has got to have a big heart.

It's such an honor to catch her hand as we walk across a road, as we have had to do for each other all these years that we have walked this journey we call life. One day we will walk hand in hand over Heaven and explore all the wonderful things waiting for us there.

Beverages

Homemade Eggnog

A wonderful, homemade eggnog. This puts store-bought eggnog to shame, and it's more than worth the extra effort! Begin 2 hours ahead of time, or early in the day. You can also make the preliminary mixture the night before if you like. If you've never had genuine, home-made eggnog, you don't know what you're missing out on!

Ingredients

- 12 eggs, separated
- 1 cup sugar
- 1 ½ cups rum
- ½ cup brandy
- 6 cups milk
- ground nutmeg
- 1 cup heavy or whipping cream

Instructions

1. In a large bowl, beat egg yolks with sugar at low speed to mix.
2. When mixed, beat at high speed until mixture is thick and lemon-colored (about 15 minutes), frequently scraping bowl.
3. Carefully beat in rum and brandy, one Tbsp. at a time to prevent curdling mixture.
4. Cover and chill. This is your base mixture and can be stored for a while until you're ready to serve the eggnog.

5. About 20 minutes before serving, in a chilled 5- to 6-quart punch bowl, stir in yolk mixture, milk and 1¼ tsp. of nutmeg.
6. In a large bowl, beat egg whites at high speed until soft peaks form.
7. In a small bowl, using the same beaters and with mixer at medium speed, beat cream until stiff peaks form.
8. With wire whisk, gently fold the egg whites and cream into your yolk mixture until just blended.
9. To serve, sprinkle some nutmeg over the top of the eggnog.

Recipe type: Beverages
Serves: 19
Prep time: 2 hrs
Cook time: 15 mins
Total time: 2 hrs 15 mins

PEACH TEA SANGRIA

Ingredients

- 2 cups water
- 3 peach teabags
- 2 tsp. sugar
- 2 cups dry red wine
- 1 green apple, cored and thinly sliced
- 1 orange, thinly sliced
- 1 lemon, thinly sliced
- 1 lime, thinly sliced
- medium saucepan
- large pitcher

Instructions

1. Bring water to a boil in medium saucepan.
2. Remove from heat.
3. Add the teabags and allow them to steep 2-3 minutes.
4. Allow to cool completely.
5. Add sugar, using more or less of it than the recipe according to taste.
6. Pour into pitcher.
7. Slice the fruit and add to the pitcher.
8. Top off the pitcher by adding the red wine.
9. Allow the flavors to blend in the refrigerator overnight or serve immediately over ice.

Recipe type: Beverages
Serves: 12
Prep time: 15 mins
Cook time: 15 mins
Total time: 30 mins

PEGGY'S SOUTHERN STYLE SWEET TEA

No meal was complete at Mama Peggy's table without some fine Southern style sweet tea. This is how the tea tasted at Peggy's Restaurant. It was served over ice, and our Northern friends would often mix a half a glass of tea with water because this Southern style tea was too sweet for them.

Ingredients

- 4 Luzianne family size tea bags
- 1 ½ cups sugar
- 1 gal. water

Instructions

1. Place tea bags in an average size saucepan and fill half full with water.
2. Bring water to a boil on stove-top.
3. Remove from heat and allow tea to "steep" for 10 or 15 minutes.
4. Add sugar to your tea pitcher (remember, this recipe is for a gallon) and pour the warm tea mixture over.
5. Stir until sugar has melted.

6. Now you have two options. The first is to just fill the rest of your tea pitcher with water, stirring as it's filled.
7. The other option, if you like stronger tea, is to pour water of the tea bags that are still in your saucepan and hold press the tea bags slightly with a spoon as you pour off the water into your tea pitcher. You can repeat this several times until the tea mixture is mostly water. Then just top off your tea pitcher with water.
8. Chill in the refrigerator and serve over ice.

Recipe type: Beverages
Serves: 16
Prep time: 5 mins
Cook time: 10 mins
Total time: 15 mins

STRAWBERRY TEA

Ingredients

- 1 cup Orange Juice
- ¼ cup sugar
- ⅓ cup powdered instant tea
- 1 (10 oz) pkg. frozen strawberries, thawed
- 4 cups water
- 2 cups crushed ice
- Fresh lemon wedges (optional)pitcher

Instructions

1. In a blender, combine orange juice, sugar, tea and strawberries.
2. Blend until smooth.
3. Pour mixture into a 2-quart pitcher.
4. Add water and ice.
5. Serve tea in tall drinking glasses and garnish with a fresh lemon wedge, if desired.

Recipe type: Beverages
Serves: 6
Prep time: 15 mins
Cook time: 0 mins
Total time: 15 mins

Peggy's Blog – The Christmas Spirit
December 20, 2008

    Everywhere you look, every time you turn on the T.V., or pick up a newspaper all you see and hear is the economy and the mess we are in. Most everyone is looking for a way out and looking to our new President to help lead the way. Even in my own family, the way seems bleak. They keep thinking this is going to be a Christmas without too many gifts.
    Well, I remember so many Christmas's when I was a little girl, we hardly knew what gifts were. We would get a bag of fruit and a small bag of candy and we were so thrilled over it. Christmas to us wasn't worry and fretting over whether or not we would get presents. It was about the birth of Jesus.
    Daddy would get up first and build a fire in the fireplace. As soon as it got warm enough, we would jump out of bed and run in there to get our fruit and candy. A happy bunch of kids we were, too! We were poor, but so was almost everyone else back then.
    I remember that my brother Robert's wife, Kate, would always send us a cardboard box with little hair-bows, small toys and such. I never forgot that!! She was so sweet to us, and still is; A woman who is in her eighties now and has worked hard all her life; Raised five sons, a wonderful mother and wife, who didn't have an easy life with our brother, who in later years let alcohol almost ruin him and his family.

There is not a one of the eleven sisters and brothers who hasn't had hard times every now and then and we may have gotten knocked down but by the Grace of a loving God, we never stayed down.

Sherry and Sue both have been depressed over the state of circumstances lately, and I will have to admit I was beginning to fill a little that way myself. But I just talked to God about it and asked Him to help us have the best Christmas ever by reminding us how far He has brought us in our lives.

Sherry just had two surgeries since May and almost lost her life both times. Sue broke her hip, which left her with a limp, but it could have killed her. She lay in her sun-room floor several hours before anyone came to her rescue BUT God was with both of them.

Libby (my best friend), her son, Warren, and I went to Charlotte Farmers Market today and dropped into Cracker Barrel for dinner. Everything was so festive and decorated for Christmas. But one young black man was walking through the front entrance handing out candy and wishing customers a Merry Christmas. He handed me some candy and laughed and asked "Did your mama not ever tell you to not take candy from a stranger?" I laughed and told him at my age it didn't matter! But you know what, after awhile I caught myself singing along with the Christmas carols and smiling along with everyone else. IT CAUGHT ON!

I told him I didn't have a dab of Christmas spirit when I walked in there and thanked him for what he was doing. He remarked that Christmas was only one day but he tried to be that way every day!

Wouldn't it be wonderful if we could just start trying to smile a little more, Hug a little more and most of all Thank

God a WHOLE lot more. For Families and friends who love us and a God who loves us MORE!

I called Sherry when I got home and told her I was tired of looking at those big brown sad eyes. That I wanted her to start remembering what God had done for her this year and what He had brought her through. Then tomorrow night we were going to take Mark with us and go to Second Baptist Church to hear Lynn (Sherry's daughter-in-law) sing in their Christmas Cantata.

I don't know what kind of Christmas you are going to have this year, but I am going to have a MERRY CHRISTMAS and a HAPPY HAPPY NEW YEAR!

Bread

Peggy's Cornbread

We almost didn't post this recipe. Making cornbread was such a simple, every day thing for Mama Peggy that she never thought about writing down a recipe. Who needs a recipe for cornbread? Well, some of us do! And here's how you can make it like Mama Peggy.

Ingredients

- 2 large eggs
- 2 cups buttermilk
- ¼ cup Crisco
- 2 cups self-rising corn meal mix
- ¼ cup all-purpose flour

Instructions

1. Heat oven to 450 degrees.
2. Coat 8 or 9-inch skillet or cornbread pan with Crisco.
3. Beat egg in medium bowl.
4. Stir in buttermilk, Crisco and corn meal mix until smooth. Batter should be pourable. If too thick, add a little more buttermilk.
5. Place the skillet or cornbread pan you prepared into the oven 7 to 8 minutes until hot (this helps with your crust).
6. Pour your prepared mixture in the skillet or pan.
7. Bake 20 to 25 minutes or until golden brown.

8. For a little extra richness, remove cornbread after it has started to rise and coat the top with butter, then place back in the oven to finish.

NOTE: If you make this with regular corn meal (meaning not self-rising), add 2 tsp. of baking powder and leave out the ¼ cup of all-purpose flour.

Recipe type: Bread
Serves: 6-8
Prep time: 5 mins
Cook time: 25 mins
Total time: 30 mins

Peggy's Southern Style Buttermilk Biscuits

One of Mama Peggy's most sought-after recipes. Everyone who knew Peggy Chaney still talks about her Southern style buttermilk biscuits. Now you can make your own.

Ingredients

- 4 cups self-rising flour
- ½ cup Crisco vegetable shortening
- 1½ cups buttermilk
- 2 tbsp melted butter, optional

Instructions

1. Heat oven to 450 degrees F.

2. Grease baking sheet with vegetable shortening.
3. Measure flour by spooning flour lightly into measuring cup.
4. Using a pastry cutter, two knives or your fingertips, cut the shortening into the flour until the pieces are about the size of peas.
5. Stir in the buttermilk until the flour is moistened. Do not over-mix. Add enough buttermilk so the dough is slightly sticky, but not wet, when touched. You'll know you have it right when the dough will come away from the bowl mostly without sticking to it (don't get the dough too wet).
6. Turn the dough onto a lightly floured surface. Shape dough into a ball using floured hands. Handle the dough as little as possible. The more you work it, the worse your biscuits will turn out. Press dough to flatten slightly and fold in half. Repeat 4-6 times.
7. Lightly roll the dough using a floured rolling pin to ½-inch thick.
8. Cut biscuits using a floured 2-inch biscuit cutter, without twisting the cutter.
9. Place biscuits on the pan so that each biscuit is touching for soft biscuits (Peggy style) or slightly apart for more crisp biscuits.
10. Put into oven and bake just until dough has started to rise (but before they've started to brown). Remove from oven and butter the tops of the biscuits.
11. Return to oven and bake for 5 to 10 minutes or until biscuits are lightly browned.

12. Remove from oven and butter tops again (optional).

Recipe type: Bread
Serves: 15
Prep time: 15 mins
Cook time: 15 mins
Total time: 30 mins

Pumpkin Bread

Ingredients

- 3 cups sugar
- 1 cup salad oil
- 1 tsp. cinnamon
- 2/3 cups water
- 2 cups cooked, unsweetened pumpkin (may use fresh or 1 lb. can)
- 2 tsp. soda
- 4 eggs
- 1 ½ tsp. salt
- 3 ½ c. flour
- 1 cup walnuts (pecans or English walnuts)

Instructions

1. Combine oil and sugar in large bowl.
2. Add eggs; beat well.
3. Combine dry ingredients and add alternately with water.
4. Mix well.
5. Add pumpkin and nuts.

6. Mix and pour into 3 small loaf pans which have been greased and floured.
7. Bake at 350 degrees for 50 to 60 minutes.
8. Test with a straw or toothpick for done-ness.
9. DO NOT OVERCOOK.
10. Allow to cool after baking and then wrap individually in foil and refrigerate.

"They are better if you don't cut them until after three days. They also freeze well! Try them as tiny sandwiches, using cream cheese between them! Very good!" ~ *Mama Peggy*

Recipe type: Bread
Serves: 6-8
Prep time: 20 mins
Cook time: 60 mins
Total time: 1 hr 20 mins

Peggy's Blog – Happy New Year!
January 1, 2009

I woke up this morning with a good feeling about this new year God has given us. Just got my feet on the floor, when the phone rang. My sister was calling and as I looked at her name on the identifier, I remembered how mad I was at her last evening at Wal-Mart. She will be eighty on January 8th. Sometimes she seems to think I am only about ten years old and must look to her. Actually, I'm only four years younger than she is.

I sat there for a moment and then picked up the phone. She already seemed to have forgotten that I was supposed to be mad at her, and she said cheerfully, "How are you feeling this morning?" For just a minute, I started to say, "I'm still mad at you" and then I thought for another minute "OH! NO! I'm not starting my new year off this way!" So, I just said "O.K." We talked for a little while and what do you know? The bad feelings subsided, and we were sisters again, who really love each other with all our hearts.

That's the way it should be for all people and then maybe we would have peace in this world! Do you realize there are sisters and brothers who have gotten mad at each over some little something and haven't spoken for years? How Sad! Listen! There was seven girls and five boys in our family, and did we fight? Absolutely! Like cats and Dogs sometimes. But there was so much love between us, that by bedtime we couldn't remember anything about it.

In this New Year I'm going try to "Live the way God wants me to live, I'm going to give, until there's no more to give, I'm going to Love, love, 'til there's just no more love, I could never out-love the Lord", as the Gaithers wrote in one of their songs.

That's going to be my only resolution this year! No use to say I'm going to lose weight. That just too laughable. I haven't been doing that but just since Kevin (MY PRECIOUS SON) was born 43 yrs. ago. See, you're laughing already. I lied about the gray hair too! My hair is now light ash brown with blond highlights. Looks pretty nifty too, for a 75 ½ year old woman. I started lining my eyes again. I will continue until my hands start shaking and I can't hit them! I feel so much better about myself already that I've actually got a skip in my step!

To get a little more on a serious side, I want to quote an author that I read in the Kings Mountain Herald this morning. He Claims he is resigning as an adult; "I have decided I would like to accept the responsibilities of a 5-year-old again. I want to go to McDonalds' and think that it is a four-star restaurant. I want to sail sticks across a fresh mud puddle and make ripples in a pond with rocks. I want to think M&M's are better than money because you can eat them. I want to lie under a big oak tree and watch the ants march up its trunk. I want to go fishing and care more about catching minnows along the shore than the big bass in the lake".

After the chaos of last year, the ugliness of a campaign, a sister being gravely ill, another friend dying from C.O.P.D., a devastating economy… I could go on and on. But be honest. Wouldn't you sometimes just like to go back to what used to be when you were small? But we can have Hope and Faith that this New Year is going to be all we think it can be.

God Is Still in Heaven and He (Regardless of what you might want to think) is in complete Control. Keep Looking Up!

Desserts - Cakes

Apple, Walnut, and Honey Spice Cake
(with Honey Cream Cheese Frosting)

We almost didn't post this recipe. Making cornbread was such a simple, every day thing for Mama Peggy that she never thought about writing down a recipe. Who needs a recipe for cornbread? Well, some of us do! And here's how you can make it like Mama Peggy.

Ingredients

- 3 large eggs, at room temperature
- ¾ cup packed light brown sugar
- 2 tsp. vanilla extract
- ¾ cup Honey
- ¾ cup vegetable oil
- 2 ½ cups unbleached all-purpose flour
- 1 tsp. each baking powder and baking soda
- 2 tsp. cinnamon
- ½ tsp. salt
- 3 cups diced, peeled and cored crisp apples (Fuji, Granny smith or Golden Delicious)
- 1 cup broken Walnuts
- 1 cup diced dried apricots or golden raisins.
- Honey Cream Cheese frosting (recipes follows)
- ½ cup finely chopped walnuts

Instructions

1. Heat oven to 350 degrees. Spray 9 x 13-inch pan with non-stick spray.

2. In a large bowl, with an electric mixer, beat eggs, brown sugar, and vanilla for 5 minutes or until light.
3. Slowly beat in honey and oil until well blended.
4. In a separate bowl, stir flour, baking powder, baking soda, cinnamon and salt together.
5. Add flour mixture, Apples, Walnuts, and apricots to egg mixture; fold together until blended.
6. Pour into prepared pan.
7. Bake 35 minutes or until top is set; cool in pan.
8. Spread with Honey Cream Cheese frosting.
9. Sprinkle with chopped walnuts.
10. Cut into squares.

Honey Cream Cheese Frosting

Beat 2 (8 oz. each) softened Cream Cheese, ½ cup Honey, and 2 tsp. vanilla extract until light and fluffy. Chill until stiff enough to spread.

Recipe type: Desserts - Cakes
Serves: 6-8
Prep time: 15 mins
Cook time: 35 mins
Total time: 50 mins

APPLESAUCE CAKE

This is the applesauce cake you want on a cool autumn Sunday evening. Full of the flavors everyone craves – brown sugar, cinnamon, ginger, and cloves. It's very moist and delicious all by itself, but even yummier with a dollop of whipped cream or frosting!

Ingredients

- 3 cups flour
- 1 tbsp baking soda
- 1 Tbsp. baking cocoa
- 1 tsp. cinnamon
- 1 tsp. cloves
- 1 tsp. allspice
- 2 cups sugar
- 3 cups applesauce
- ¼ cup butter, softened
- 1 cup chopped pecans
- 1 cup raisins
- Frosting

Instructions

1. Combine flour, soda, baking cocoa, cinnamon, cloves and allspice in a large bowl; mix well.
2. Mix sugar with applesauce (If you use store-bought applesauce, choose one with a chunky texture) in bowl; mix well.
3. Stir in butter, pecans and raisins.
4. Pour into 3 greased and floured 9-inch cake pans.

5. Bake at 350 degrees for 25-30 minutes or until layers are done.
6. Remove to wire racks to cool.
7. Spread frosting between layers and over top and side of cake.

FROSTING:

1½ cups sugar, 1 20 oz. can crushed pineapple, 1 7 oz can coconut, 1 tbsp flour - Combine ingredients in saucepan. Cook until thickened, stirring constantly.

Recipe type: Desserts - Cakes
Serves: 12
Prep time: 15 mins
Cook time: 30 mins
Total time: 45 mins

Carrot Layer Cake

Ingredients

- 2 cups sugar
- 1 ½ Cup oil
- 4 eggs – well beaten
- 2 tsp. baking soda
- 2 cups all-purpose flour
- 2 tsp. cinnamon
- 1 cup chopped pecans
- 3 cups carrots-grated

Instructions

1. Mix sugar and oil together.
2. Add eggs and mix well.
3. Combine dry ingredients and stir into sugar mixture.
4. Mix until smooth.
5. Add pecans and carrots.
6. Bake in 3 greased 9-inch layer cake pans at 350 degrees for 25 to 30 minutes!
7. Cool and frost.

Frosting:

- 1 box powdered sugar
- 8 oz. cream cheese
- ½ stick butter
- 1 tsp. lemon extract

Recipe type: Desserts - Cakes
Serves: 8-10
Prep time: 15 mins
Cook time: 30 mins
Total time: 45 mins

COLD OVEN POUND CAKE

Ingredients

- 3 cups plain flour
- 2 sticks margarine
- 1 cup milk
- 1 ½ tsp. vanilla flavoring
- 3 cups sugar
- ½ cup Crisco
- 5 large eggs
- 1 ½ tsp. lemon flavoring

Instructions

1. Cream margarine and Crisco.
2. Add sugar, beat in eggs one at a time.
3. Add flour and milk alternately.
4. Add flavorings.
5. Pour into greased and floured tube pan.
6. Place in cold oven.
7. Bake at 375 degrees for 1 ½ hours.

Recipe type: Desserts - Cakes
Serves: 8-10
Prep time: 15 mins
Cook time: 1 hr 30 mins
Total time: 1 hr 45 mins

Dream Cake

Ingredients

- ½ cup dark brown sugar
- 1 cup butter or margarine
- 2 cups all-purpose flour
- 1 tsp. vanilla

Filling

- 4 eggs
- 3 cups brown sugar
- 2 tsp. vanilla
- ¼ to ½ cup of all-purpose flour
- 2 tsp. baking powder
- 1 ½ cups flaked coconut
- 2 cups chopped pecans

Instructions

1. Preheat oven to 350 degrees.
2. Use a pastry blender to combine the crust ingredients.
3. Press the mixture into a greased 9 x 13-inch baking pan.
4. Bake for 10 minutes.
5. Meanwhile, beat 4 eggs well.
6. Add other ingredients, stir well.
7. Then pour the filling over the baked crust and bake at 350 degrees for 45 to 60 minutes.
8. Let cool, then cut into squares.

9. Best with a scoop of French vanilla ice cream.

Recipe type: Desserts - Cakes
Serves: 8-10
Prep time: 20 mins
Cook time: 1 hr 10 mins
Total time: 1 hr 30 mins

OLD-FASHIONED BLACK WALNUT POUND CAKE

Here's a recipe that any old-time Southern cook has to have in her collection. This is a black walnut pound cake recipe like our grandmothers used to make, and is at least 100 years old. You can serve this cake with or without an icing, but it's amazing by itself. Nothing beats a nice, warm slice of old fashioned black walnut cake on a chilly autumn day. Enjoy!

Ingredients

- ½ lb. margarine or butter
- ½ cup Crisco
- 5 eggs
- 3 cups plain flour
- 3 cups sugar
- 1 tsp. vanilla
- 1 tsp. baking powder
- ½ tsp. black walnut flavoring
- 1 cup evaporated milk
- 1 cup chopped black walnuts

Instructions

1. Cream margarine/butter and shortening.
2. Add sugar and beat until light and fluffy.
3. Add eggs, one at a time, and beat well.
4. Add flavoring and beat well.
5. Mix ¼ cup of flour with nuts, and sift remaining flour with baking powder and alternately add with milk, starting and ending with flour.
6. Fold in floured nuts. Do not beat!
7. Bake in greased and floured tube pan for 1 hour and 20 minutes in 325-degree oven.

Recipe type: Desserts - Cakes
Serves: 12
Prep time: 20 mins
Cook time: 1 hr 20 mins
Total time: 1 hr 40 mins

Old Fashioned Lemon Pound Cake

This is the perfect pound cake for folks who like a little of that lemon zing. It's not as super-sweet as most of the lemon pound cake recipes out there.

Ingredients

- ½ lb. butter
- ½ cup shortening
- 3 cups sugar
- 6 eggs
- 1 tsp. baking powder
- 1 cup milk
- 1 tsp. vanilla
- 1 tsp. lemon flavoring
- 3 cups flour

Instructions

8. Grease and flour a tube pan.
9. Cream butter, shortening, and sugar.
10. Add eggs one at a time, beating well after each egg added.
11. Mix in the vanilla and the milk.
12. Sift in the dry ingredients.
13. Pour mixture into pan and place on low rack in a cold oven.
14. Bake at 325 degrees for 1½ hours.
15. If you want a glaze, just mix 1¼ cups powdered sugar, 2 tsp. lemon juice, and 1 to 2 Tbsp. milk, and pour over top of the cooled cake.

Recipe type: Desserts - Cakes
Serves: 8
Prep time: 15 mins
Cook time: 1 hr 30 mins
Total time: 1 hr 45 mins

ORANGE CRUSH POUND CAKE

Ingredients

- 2 ¾ cups sugar
- 1 cup vegetable shortening
- 1 stick butter or margarine
- 5 eggs
- 3 cups cake flour (if you use all-purpose flour, you must sift it four times)
- ½ tsp. salt
- 1 cup Orange Crush soda
- 1 tsp. orange flavoring
- 1 tsp. vanilla flavoring

Instructions

1. Preheat oven to 350 degrees.
2. Beat sugar and shortening until fluffy.
3. Add eggs, one at a time, beating well after each addition.
4. Add dry ingredients alternately with the Orange Crush.
5. Add flavorings.
6. Pour into greased and floured tube pan.
7. Bake for 1 hour and ten minutes.

8. Let cake cool about 15 minutes.
9. Spread frosting on cake while it's still warm!

Frosting:

Ingredients

- 1 (3 oz.) pkg. Cream Cheese, softened
- 1 cup powdered sugar
- ½ tsp. vanilla flavoring
- ½ tsp. orange flavoring

Instructions

1. Mix well until spreadable.

Recipe type: Desserts - Cakes
Serves: 8
Prep time: 15 mins
Cook time: 1 hr 10 mins
Total time: 1 hr 25 mins

PEANUT BUTTER CHOCOLATE CAKE

Ingredients

- 2 cups all-purpose flour
- 2 cups sugar
- ⅔ cup baking cocoa
- 2 tsp. baking soda
- 1 tsp. baking powder
- ½ tsp. salt
- 2 eggs
- 1 cup milk
- ⅔ cup vegetable oil
- 1 tsp. vanilla extract
- 1 cup brewed coffee, room temperature

Peanut Butter Frosting

- 1 pkg. (3 oz.) cream cheese, softened
- ¼ cup creamy peanut butter
- 2 cups confectioners' sugar
- 2 Tbsp. milk
- ½ tsp. vanilla extract
- miniature semisweet chocolate chips

Instructions

1. In a mixing bowl, combine dry ingredients.
2. Add eggs, milk, oil and vanilla; beat for 2 minutes.
3. Stir in coffee (batter will be thin).
4. Pour into a greased 13 x 9 x 2-inch baking pan.

5. Bake at 350 degrees for 30-40 minutes or until a wooden pick inserted near the center comes out clean.
6. Cool completely on a wire rack.
7. For frosting, beat the cream cheese and peanut butter in a mixing bowl until smooth.
8. Beat in sugar, milk and vanilla.
9. Spread over cake.
10. Sprinkle with chocolate chips, if desired.
11. Serves 16-20.

Recipe type: Desserts - Cakes
Serves: 10-12
Prep time: 25 mins
Cook time: 40 mins
Total time: 1 hr 5 mins

Pineapple Coconut Cake

Ingredients

- 5 eggs, separated
- 1 can (20 oz.) crushed pineapple
- 1 ½ cups all-purpose flour
- 2 ½ tsp. baking powder
- 1 ¼ cups sugar, divided
- ¼ cup butter, melted
- 2 tsp. coconut flavoring
- 1 tsp. vanilla flavoring

Icing

- 4 cups of heavy cream (whipping)
- 1 ½ cups of powdered sugar, divided
- 2 pkg. (8 oz. each) cream cheese, softened
- 5 cups of flaked coconut, divided

Instructions

1. Place egg whites in a large bowl; let stand at room temperature for 30 minutes.
2. Drain pineapple, reserving 1 cup juice. Set aside.
3. In a small bowl, combine flour and baking powder.
4. In another bowl, beat egg yolks until slightly thickened.
5. Gradually add 1 cup sugar, beating on high speed until thick and lemon colored.
6. Beat in the butter, flavorings and ½ cup reserved juice.

7. Add dry ingredients; beat until well blended.
8. Beat egg whites with clean beaters on medium speed until soft peaks form.
9. Gradually add remaining sugar, 1 Tbsp. at a time, beating on high until stiff peaks form.
10. Fold into batter.
11. Transfer to two greased and floured 9-inch round cake pans.
12. Bake at 350 degrees for 18 to 22 minutes or until cake springs back when lightly touched.
13. Cool for ten minutes before removing from pans to cool completely.
14. In a large bowl whip cream until it begins to thicken.
15. Add 1 cup powdered sugar and beat until stiff peaks form.
16. In another bowl, beat the cream cheese, pineapple and remaining powdered sugar until blended: Stir in two cups coconut.
17. Fold in whipped cream, cover and refrigerate for at least an hour.
18. Cut each cake horizontally into two layers!
19. Place bottom layer on serving plate; drizzle with two Tbsp. reserved juice.
20. Spread with 2 cups icing.
21. Repeat layers twice.
22. Top with remaining cake layer and drizzle with remaining juice.
23. Spread remaining icing over top and sides of cake.
24. Press remaining coconut onto top and sides.
25. Refrigerate for at least one hour before serving!!! Enjoy!!!!

Recipe type: Desserts - Cakes
Serves: 10-12
Prep time: 45 mins
Cook time: 22 mins
Total time: 1 hr 7 mins

PINEAPPLE COCONUT LAYER CAKE

Ingredients

- 1 pkg. yellow cake mix.
- ⅓ cup oil
- 3 eggs
- 1 tsp. vanilla
- 1 cup milk
- ¼ cup pineapple juice

Instructions

1. Mix and bake in 2 layers, according to directions on the package.
2. When cake layers are cold, split in half to make four layers.
3. Mix the following:
    - 1 cup sugar
    - 1 cup sour cream
    - 1 cup pineapple, well drained coconut
4. Put ¼ of the mixture on three layers and sprinkle with thawed frozen coconut.
5. When you get the cake assembled, spread sides and top with Cool whip.
6. Then sprinkle coconut over all!

"Try it! You'll love it!" ~ *Mama Peggy*

Recipe type: Desserts - Cakes
Serves: 10-12
Prep time: 20 mins
Cook time: 30 mins
Total time: 50 mins

PUMPKIN PECAN CAKE

Ingredients

- 2 cups crushed vanilla wafers (about 50)
- 1 cup chopped pecans
- ¾ cup butter or margarine, softened

Cake

- 1 box (18 ¼ oz.) spice cake mix
- 1 can (16 oz.) solid-pack pumpkin
- ¼ cup butter or margarine, softened
- 4 eggs

Filling/Topping

- ⅔ cup butter or margarine, softened
- 1 package (3 oz.) cream cheese, softened
- 3 cups confectioners' sugar
- 2 tsp. vanilla extract
- ½ cup caramel ice cream topping

Instructions

1. In a mixing bowl on medium speed, beat the wafers, pecans and butter until crumbly, about 1 minute.
2. Press into three greased and floured 9 in. round cake pans.
3. In another mixing bowl, beat cake mix, pumpkin, butter and eggs.
4. Spread over crust in each pan.
5. Bake at 350 degrees for 30 minutes or until a wooden toothpick inserted in the center comes out clean.
6. Cool in pans 10 minutes; remove to wire racks and cool completely.
7. For filling: combine butter and cream cheese in a small mixing bowl.
8. Add vanilla and sugar; beat on medium until light and fluffy, about 3 minutes.
9. Thinly spread between layers (crumb side down) and on the sides of cake.
10. Spread caramel topping over the top of cake, allowing some to drip down the sides.
11. Store in refrigerator. Makes 16 to 20 servings.

Recipe type: Desserts - Cakes
Serves: 12-14
Prep time: 20 mins
Cook time: 30 mins
Total time: 50 mins

SOUTHERN PINEAPPLE POUND CAKE

Ingredients

- ½ cup Crisco
- 2 sticks butter
- 2 ¾ cup sugar
- 6 large Eggs
- 3 cups sifted plain flour
- 1 tsp. baking powder
- ¼ cup milk
- 1 tsp. vanilla
- ¾ cup undrained crushed pineapple

Instructions

1. Cream shortening and butter: add sugar.
2. Add eggs, one at a time, beating well after each addition.
3. Add sifted flour with baking powder, alternately with milk.
4. Add vanilla.
5. Stir in pineapple and blend well.
6. Pour into greased and floured 10-inch tube pan.
7. Place in cold oven and set oven to 325 degrees.
8. Cook 1 ½ hours or until the top springs back.
9. Let cool 5 minutes. Then run knife around pan and remove.

Glaze:

- ¼ cup butter
- 1 ¼ cups confectioners' sugar
- ½ cup well drained crushed pineapple

Instructions

1. Place pineapple in blender for a second or two.
2. Combine with other ingredients and pour over cake while it is still hot!

Recipe type: Desserts - Cakes
Serves: 12-14
Prep time: 20 mins
Cook time: 1 hr 30 mins
Total time: 1 hr 50 mins

SWEET POTATO POUND CAKE

Ingredients

- 1 cup butter
- 2 cups sugar
- 2 ½ cups cooked mashed sweet potatoes
- 4 eggs
- 3 cups flour (all purpose)
- ¼ tsp. salt
- 2 tsp. baking powder
- 1 tsp. baking soda
- ½ tsp. nutmeg

- 1 tsp. cinnamon
- 1 tsp. vanilla
- ½ cup coconut
- ½ cup pecans (I used walnuts. They were fine)

Instructions

1. Cream butter and sugar until fluffy; beat in potatoes.
2. Add eggs, one at a time.
3. Combine the flour, salt, baking powder, soda, nutmeg, and cinnamon; stir into creamed mixture.
4. Add vanilla and mix well.
5. Stir in nuts and coconut.
6. Spoon into greased and floured tube pan.
7. Bake at 350 degrees for 1 ¼ hours or until done.
8. Combine the following icing ingredients and spread over the hot cake.

Glaze:

- Grated rind of 1 orange
- Juice and rind of 1 lemon
- 1 box of powdered sugar

Recipe type: Desserts - Cakes
Serves: 12-14
Prep time: 15 mins
Cook time: 1 hr 15 mins
Total time: 1 hr 30 mins

Peggy's Blog – Loretta, My Best Friend
January 4, 2009

Today would have been Lo's 74th birthday. I was one year and eight months older than she was. From the time we were small, where you saw one of us, you saw the other. We loved each other so much and always had such a strong bond.

For some reason, I felt more like her second mama than anything else. I always looked after her. But of course, as we grew up and older, we sort of went our separate ways. I got married. She and our older sister Dot, or "Sis" as we all called her, moved in together. After six years my marriage was over and I moved in with them, along with my 5 yr. old son, Kevin. We all worked at a little restaurant called Piedmont Lunch.

We were never allowed to dance, since our Dad was a very strict Baptist minister. Lo, Sis, Billie Hoyle (a lifelong friend) had been going to Charlotte, N.C. to dances at some of the nicer lounges. They talked me into going with them and I was carried away by the music and watching people dance. I loved it, although I couldn't dance myself. Every time the music started, here would come a guy asking Lo to dance. I would never have believed that girl could dance like that. Sis could dance real good, too! Slowly but surely I got up the nerve to try it. I learned to slow dance but would never have had the nerve to try that fast music.

Then a year later, I married Jim Childers. He was a customer who came in the restaurant where we three worked. His wife had died, leaving him with two children to finish raising (That's my story, THAT I will tackle at another time). Loretta, Sis and Billie had all married. Somehow we all seemed to choose the wrong men. Sis went to Georgia to live with her daughter, Teresa. Billie had a thriving beauty shop. Loretta lived with her husband Bill about a block from us (me & Jim). Jim had bought Piedmont Lunch and changed the name to Peggy's Restaurant. He wouldn't allow me to work, so I suggested that he sell it to Lo. He did so and she later moved it about a block down the street. She had a booming business there, with a lot of family members working for her. Our cousin, Rene Smith, was the cook, Lo helped on the grill when she was needed, and Sherry, our youngest sister was one of the waitresses along with Sis.

After a few years, Kevin was about 11 yrs. old, Sis had to go to Georgia to spend some time and Lo called and asked me to fill in for Sis. I did and Lo came to me one day and said, "you seem so happy working, why don't you try it for a while?" Terry, my step daughter, was married. Chip (my stepson) was 16, so I decided to take the job. I just didn't have enough to do at home. It was a hard job, but we had a ball! Our customers were like family. They would get up from their tables and pour coffee, clean tables, all kinds of things.

Well, the way my luck with men went, I found out that my husband Jim was being unfaithful to me with his secretary, Pat! So, another divorce was in the works.

I worked at the restaurant and cooked (after Rene died) until I retired 23 years later. I could sit here all night talking about Lo and how much I loved her. Kevin and I moved back in with her again after my divorce. We were as content as two sisters could be together. Again, just as it was in the beginning we were inseparable. She would be in her room at night, and I in mine watching television. Or going shopping, running back and forth to one of our sister's houses. Working in the backyard in our flowers, me digging and Lo picking up the weeds and cleaning up after me.

Sis learned that she had lung cancer and I made the choice to go to Georgia to take care of her. Lo came down to stay with us for a week. She was thin and very pale. My sister Sue, who was also there, said to me "If I had to say which one would go first, by the way they look, I would have to say Loretta". I will never forget the day she left to go back home. I stood in the door and she turned back and was staring at me, with the saddest look I have ever seen. Like she was saying "I want you to go with me". I couldn't because Sis was nearing death. Sis died a few weeks later. We brought her back to Kings Mountain to bury her beside Mama and Daddy.

The day we drove up the drive way, Loretta came running out the door and she said, "I have been lying here all day waiting for you to get home".

Then two months Later, Lo and I had been piddling in the back yard, trying to get things back in shape. We came in for a little while and decided to go to McDonalds to get a sandwich. Lo was behind me and we were laughing at Stripe, one of our cats, who was laying in a concrete basket asleep. I opened the door to get in the van and looked around to the passenger seat and didn't see Lo. I looked back and saw her sitting on the sidewalk crying with her leg. She said I hit her with the door as I opened it, but I felt no contact as I opened the door. I ran in the house and called the paramedics. While they were taking her to the hospital, they had to give her oxygen because her oxygen reading was just

40. The doctor came out and told us they would like to keep Lo overnight because she had broken her leg pretty bad.

The next morning, I went to the Hospital early, expecting that they would set her leg and we would be on our way home. But the Dr. came in and told us that he had no good news; that Loretta had an enlarged heart, very little circulation in her legs, and a very large aneurysm on the tube going in to her stomach. He said they were afraid to set her leg because they were afraid of a blood clot. Lo and I just said there wide eyed and didn't know what to say. The next day they gave her a drug induced stress test and her heart stopped. They worked on her until her heart began beating again, but she had to spend two days in ICU. Dr. ____ (the heart specialist) came in and talked to us the next day. He told us he didn't want to send her home with that leg not in a cast because she would have to stay in bed and be in pain the rest of her life. He told us he would take care of the aneurysm when she got over the rest.

She did well and the next Tuesday morning we brought her home. On the fifth day at home, she told me she was having chest pains. I called the paramedics and she made them believe that she had a Hiatal hernia and hadn't chewed her food well at breakfast. They left and at the same time Kevin told me someone wanted me on the telephone. I was on the phone no more than 10 minutes and then I hurried back to Loretta. I touched her on the foot and it felt funny. I looked at her and she was gone!!!!! I screamed for Kevin and he ran in and tried to revive her, but it was too late. The paramedics came flying back to our house, along with a nurse and two ambulances. Another man was walking around in the front yard talking on a walkie talkie. BUT my sister that I loved so much was dead. I cried all night and begged the Lord to take me too! My heart still gets heavy anytime I think of her, but she made her peace with God when she was first in the hospital. She is with the rest of our family, our mama, daddy, three brothers, four sisters, counting Lo. One day I will join them in Heaven and nothing can ever separate me and Lo again. That's going to be some home coming isn't it? Keep looking Lo! One of these days you are going to see me running through those gates with my arms wide open to hug you again. Thank you, God, for that promise.

Desserts - Candy & Cookies

Cathedral Windows Candy
(Very Good! And Pretty Too!)

Cathedral windows were a seasonal favorite of Mama Peggy, and they're such a pretty Christmas candy. They accent any cookie arrangement or candy display perfectly and add a little extra colorful Christmas joy.

Ingredients

- 1 pkg. 6 oz. semi-sweet Chocolate morsels
- 2 Tbsp. margarine
- 1 egg - beaten
- 1 small pkg. miniature colored marshmallows (or ½ of a 10 oz. pkg. for 1 batch)
- ½ cup chopped pecans
- Angel Flake coconut – 7 oz. size for one batch.

Instructions

1. Melt margarine and chocolate over hot water.
2. When melted, remove from heat and add beaten egg. If too thin, put back over water and cook a little more.
3. After this mix is close to room temperature, add the nuts.
4. Stir well, then add marshmallows.
5. Stir well.
6. Spread coconut on wax paper.
7. Dip by spoonfuls onto coconut.
8. Shape into 2 long rolls (logs).

9. Refrigerate until set and then slice.

Recipe type: Desserts – Candy & Cookies
Serves: 12
Prep time: 15 mins
Cook time: 15 mins
Total time: 30 mins

Double Chocolate Peanut Butter Bars

Ingredients

- 1 cup firmly packed brown sugar
- ½ cup margarine, softened
- ½ cup chunky peanut butter
- 2 eggs
- 1 tsp. vanilla
- 1 ¾ cups all-purpose flour
- ½ tsp. baking powder
- ¼ tsp. baking soda
- 1 cup mini real semi-sweet chocolate chips
- 2 Tbsp. sugar
- 35 milk chocolate candy kisses

Instructions

1. Heat oven to 350 degrees.
2. Line a 13 × 9-inch pan with aluminum foil, leaving a 1 inch overhang; Set aside.
3. Combine brown sugar, margarine, and peanut butter in large bowl.

4. Beat at medium speed, scraping bowl often, until creamy.
5. Add eggs and vanilla; continue beating until well mixed.
6. Reduce speed to low; add flour, baking powder, and baking soda.
7. Beat until well mixed.
8. Stir in chocolate chips.
9. Pat dough into prepared pan.
10. Sprinkle with sugar.
11. Bake for 20 to 22 minutes or until golden brown.
12. Immediately press evenly spaced chocolate candies into warm bars.
13. Cool completely.
14. Remove bars from pan using edges of foil.
15. Cut into bars, cutting between candies.

Recipe type: Desserts - Candy & Cookies
Serves: 35
Prep time: 15 mins
Cook time: 22 mins
Total time: 37 mins

Dulce De Leche Bars

Ingredients

- 1 ½ cups all-purpose flour
- 1 ½ cups quick cooking oatmeal
- 1 cup packed brown sugar
- ¼ tsp. salt
- 1 cup butter
- 1 can Dulce De Leche
- 1 cup toffee bits.

Instructions

1. Heat oven to 350 degrees
2. In a large bowl, mix flour, oatmeal, brown sugar and salt.
3. Cut in butter until mixture is crumbly.
4. Press ¾ of the mixture in the bottom of 13×9-inch pan, ungreased.
5. Bake 10 minutes.
6. Meanwhile, in a 1-quart saucepan, heat Dulce De Leche over low heat 3-4 minutes, stirring frequently until it is slightly softened.
7. Spread Dulce De Leche over crust.
8. Sprinkle with toffee bits and remaining crumb mixture.
9. Return to oven and bake 20-25 minutes.
10. Cool 15 minutes, then run knife around sides of the pan.
11. Cool another 30 minutes before cutting into bars.

Note: You can find cans of dulce de leche (caramelized sweetened condensed milk) in the Latino section of most grocery stores.

Recipe type: Desserts - Candy & Cookies
Serves: 35
Prep time: 15 mins
Cook time: 35 mins
Total time: 50 mins

MACADAMIA MACAROONS

Ingredients

- 1 pkg. (7 oz.) Baker's Angel Flake coconut
- 1 cup Planters Macadamia nuts (chopped)
- 1 can (14 oz.) sweetened condensed milk
- 1 tsp. vanilla
- 30 Premium saltine crackers, finely crushed
- 3 egg whites
- 2 squares Baker's semi-sweet baking chocolate

Instructions

1. Preheat oven to 350 degrees.
2. Spread coconut and macadamias into 15 x 10 x 1-inch baking pan.
3. Bake 10 minutes until lightly toasted, and be sure to stir frequently. Cool.
4. Combine milk and vanilla in large bowl.
5. Add coconut mixture and cracker crumbs. Mix well.

6. Beat egg whites in small bowl with electric mixer on high speed until stiff peaks form.
7. Add to coconut mixture.
8. Stir gently until well blended.
9. Drop rounded Tbsp. of the coconut mixture, 2 inches apart, on lightly greased baking sheets.
10. Bake 12 to 14 minutes or until edges of cookies are lightly browned.
11. Remove to wire racks; cool completely.
12. Melt chocolate as directed on package; drizzle over cookies.
13. Place into a shallow, wax paper-lined pan.
14. Refrigerate until chocolate is set.

Recipe type: Desserts - Candy & Cookies
Serves: 20
Prep time: 15 mins
Cook time: 34 mins
Total time: 49 mins

Peanut Butter Fudge

Ingredients

- 2 cups sugar
- 1 cup evaporated milk
- 1 (12 oz.) jar of peanut butter
- 3 Tbsp. butter
- 1 cup miniature marshmallows
- 1 tsp. vanilla

Instructions

1. Add the sugar, butter, and canned milk to heavy saucepan.
2. Bring to a full, rolling boil.
3. Boil for about 6 minutes.
4. Remove from heat.
5. Add marshmallows, peanut butter, and vanilla.
6. Mix thoroughly.
7. Pour into a buttered dish, about 9 inches square.
8. Let it cool completely, and then cut into squares.

Recipe type: Desserts - Candy & Cookies
Serves: 12 – 16
Prep time: 10 mins
Cook time: 7 mins
Total time: 17 mins

Peanut Butter Rice Krispie Treats

Ingredients

- 1 Tbsp. butter
- 1 cup peanut butter
- 1 lg. pack marshmallows
- 4 ½ cups Rice Krispies
- ½ cup oats
- ½ cup dried fruit

Instructions

1. Put butter, peanut butter and marshmallows in pan over low heat and melt.
2. Add Rice Krispies, oats and dried fruit.
3. Mix well.
4. Pour into pan and allow to set up.
5. Cut into squares.
6. Drizzle melted chocolate chips over the top if you like.

Recipe type: Desserts - Candy & Cookies
Serves: 12
Prep time: 15 mins
Cook time: 30 mins
Total time: 45 mins

Pecan Pie Bars

Ingredients

- 2 ½ cups self-rising flour
- 1 cup cold butter, cut in pieces
- ½ cups sugar
- ½ tsp. salt

Topping

- 4 eggs
- 1 ½ cups light or dark corn syrup
- 1 ½ cups sugar
- 3 Tbsp. melted butter
- 1 ½ tsp. vanilla
- 2 ½ cups coarsely chopped pecans

Instructions

1. Heat oven to 350 degrees.
2. Grease 13 x 9-inch pan.
3. With a mixer at medium speed, mix ingredients until crumbly.
4. Press into bottom of pan.
5. Bake 20 -23 minutes.
6. Meanwhile, in same bowl, beat eggs, corn syrup, sugar, butter and vanilla well until blended.
7. Stir in pecans by hand.
8. Pour over hot crust and bake 25 minutes.
9. Cool completely before cutting.

Recipe type: Desserts - Candy & Cookies
Serves: 12
Prep time: 15 mins
Cook time: 25 mins
Total time: 40 mins

Peggy's Blog – Valentine's Day
January 13, 2009

Now's the time of year again when the Florist's shops are working overtime to take orders and send flowers to sweethearts, wives, and you name it.

It makes your mind wander back to some other time, some other place. The one time I remember distinctly is the first Valentine's Day after Jim and I had been married for a little over two months. Guess what I got! A box of Ayds candy. For those who don't remember what that was, it was candy that was supposed to help you lose weight. I should have kicked him to the curb then because that should have given me an inkling of what my life with him was going to be like.

The sweetest gift, I have ever received is a little dog, with red ears, a red nose and a red ring around one eye. When you turn him on, the music to "Sugar pie, Honey bunch, you know that I love you, I can't help myself, I love you and nobody else." His ears start jumping up and down and he moves his little head in time to the music! I nearly had a fit! I went to every apartment and showed and played it, for every one of the residents in our building. I have never seen such pleasure shown by all these old folks. Room no. 2 is a lady of 77 yrs. who has had one leg removed, is diabetic and also has a heart problem. She laughed until the tears came, and said that was the cutest thing she had ever seen.

The next apartment has a resident that keeps pretty much to herself. I've known her most of my life and she has always been a recluse, of sorts. But I have never seen such a smile when she saw that little dog and heard the music. She just took it in her arms and hugged it and told me she just loved it!

Then I stopped at my sister's apartment. She hasn't had much to smile about in the last year because of her illness and near-death experience. But she was smiling when I left her, also! Everyone got such a kick out of my little Valentine present.

Then on to Libby's apartment. She is my best friend, who is dying from C.O.P.D. She also, just doubled up with laughter. Zeke, her dog made a dive for my doggie, because he loves stuffed animals. I had to grab it fast to keep him from getting it.

Older people get lonely! I wish their children and friends would remember that. Betty had a misunderstanding with her three children, so they very rarely come to see her. They don't see the falling tears that I see when I drop in on her. She sits by that window most of the time. Thankfully we have a beautiful Senior Center in Kings Mountain. We are so lucky that it is only a couple blocks from where our Senior Complex is. The bus comes by here from there, to pick up anyone who wants to go, every day!

My heart was full and running over when I returned to my apartment. Who would have thought a little stuffed dog that Victoria and Kevin sent to me on Valentine's Day could have brought that much joy to so many?!

God uses people in all kinds of ways to bless His children. Betty's children might not care about her, but God does! Who knows what kind of day each one of these people had or how lonely they had been! But God knew, and He led my "munchkins", Kevin and Victoria, to that little dog. I got my special blessing by watching the faces of my neighbors as they watched a little stuffed dog do its "stuff".

Victoria and Kevin both have a store on eBay, where they sell shirts. Victoria also sent me two beautiful Tee shirts. I get to wear them and show them off to my friends. I'm looking forward to visiting them before too long, and helping them build some flower beds.

Thanks kids, for allowing God to use you to bless a bunch of "old ladies". WE Love you!

Desserts - Pies

Baked Chocolate Pie

Who doesn't love chocolate pie? But if you've only had store-bought chocolate pie, you don't know what you're missing. This old-fashioned baked chocolate pie recipe will quickly become a favorite of your family, and a dessert your kids will tell their kids about.

Ingredients

- 1 cup sugar
- 2 tbsp all-purpose flour
- 3 eggs (slightly beaten)
- ½ cup butter
- 2 blocks baker's chocolate
- 1 tsp. vanilla
- 1 cup milk

Instructions

1. Melt butter in a saucepan at low to medium-low heat.
2. Break up first block of baker's chocolate and stir into butter until melted; repeat with second block.
3. Stir in the rest of the ingredients, one at a time and mix well.
4. Pour into pie crust.
5. Bake for 45 minutes at 350 degrees.

Recipe type: Desserts - Pies
Serves: 8 – 10
Prep time: 20 mins
Cook time: 45 mins
Total time: 1 hr 5 mins

BEST PECAN PIE
(I have ever tasted)

"Wonderful pie and easy too! Try it! You'll like it! I'll bet you!!!" ~ *Mama Peggy*

Ingredients

- ½ cup butter, melted
- 1 (16 oz.) box light brown sugar
- 2 Tbsp. cornmeal
- 2 Tbsp. water
- 1 Tbsp. vanilla
- 4 eggs
- 2 cups pecans, broken
- 2 unbaked pie shells

Instructions

1. Melt butter and mix (by hand) with sugar, corn meal, water, vanilla and eggs.
2. Add pecan pieces.
3. Pour into unbaked pie shells.
4. Bake at 325 degrees for 45 minutes.

Recipe type: Desserts - Pies
Serves: 10
Prep time: 10 mins
Cook time: 45 mins
Total time: 55 mins

Cherry Pie

If you've never eaten a fresh cherry pie, you're in for a treat. It's a bit of work to pit the cherries, but once that's done, there isn't much left to do.

Ingredients

- Pastry for 2-crust pie
- 1 cup sugar
- ¼ cup cornstarch
- ½ tsp. salt
- 5 cups pitted fresh or canned tart cherries
- 1 Tbsp. butter

Instructions

1. Prepare pastry. Roll out half of pastry and line 9-inch pie plate.
2. Preheat oven to 425 degrees.
3. For filling, combine sugar, cornstarch, salt and pitted cherries.
4. Place filling in pie crust and dot with butter.
5. Roll out remaining pastry for top crust and cut a few slashes for vent.
6. Top pie with slashed top crust.

7. Flute edges.
8. Back 50-60 minutes until golden.

Recipe type: Desserts - Pies
Serves: 6
Prep time: 20 mins
Cook time: 60 mins
Total time: 1 hr 20 mins

CINNAMON STREUSEL SWEET POTATO PIE

"Since Thanksgiving is just around the corner, I thought I would post some scrumptious dessert recipes! I hope you will try a few! They are very good! I love sweet potato pies! This is a different version but very good!"
~ Mama Peggy

Ingredients

- 1 ½ cups mashed cooked dark orange sweet potatoes (about 1 lb. uncooked)
- ½ cup packed brown sugar
- 2 Tbsp. corn syrup
- 1 cup evaporated milk
- 3 eggs
- 1 tsp. ground cinnamon
- ½ tsp. ground nutmeg
- ⅛ tsp. ground cloves
- ⅛ tsp. ground ginger

Crust:

- 1 Pet-Ritz frozen deep pie crust

Streusel:

- ¼ cup brown sugar
- 2 Tbsp. all-purpose flour
- 2 Tbsp. butter or margarine
- ¼ tsp. ground cinnamon
- ¼ cup chopped pecans
- ¼ cup chopped walnuts

Topping:

- 1 cup Cool Whip, if desired.

Instructions

1. Place cookie sheet on oven rack.
2. Heat oven to 425 degrees.
3. Place sweet potatoes in food processor; cover and process until smooth.
4. In a large bowl, mix sweet potatoes and remaining filling ingredients with wire whisk until smooth.
5. Pour into frozen pie crust.
6. Bake on cookie sheet 15 minutes.
7. Reduce oven temperature to 350 degrees.
8. Bake 20 minutes longer.
9. Meanwhile, in small bowl, mix streusel ingredients. Carefully sprinkle streusel over filling.

10. Bake 10 to 15 minutes longer or until knife inserted in center comes out clean and streusel is golden brown.
11. Cool completely (about 3 hours).
12. Serve pie with Cool Whip! Store covered in refrigerator! Enjoy!

Recipe type: Desserts - Pies
Serves: 8
Prep time: 20 mins
Cook time: 50 mins
Total time: 1 hr 10 mins

COCONUT PIE

"I tell you folks, there's nothing I like better than a homemade coconut pie! The bought ones are delicious, but I don't know why, homemade ones have a different something!! Maybe thoughts of your mama and the ones she made! I thought no one could beat my mama's cooking! Enjoy!" ~ *Mama Peggy*

Ingredients

- 2 eggs
- 1 ¼ cups sugar
- ½ stick butter
- ½ cup milk
- 1 tbsp flour
- 1 tsp. vanilla
- Dash salt
- 1 can Angel flake coconut

- 1 unbaked pie shell

Instructions

1. Mix ingredients and pour into pie shell.
2. Bake at 350 degrees until slightly brown.
3. Then lower heat to 300 degrees and finish baking 50 to 60 minutes, until done.

Recipe type: Desserts - Pies
Serves: 6-8
Prep time: 10 mins
Cook time: 1 hr 10 mins
Total time: 1 hr 20 mins

CRUMB, APPLE AND PUMPKIN PIE

Ingredients

- 1 sheet refrigerated pie pastry
- 2 cups thinly sliced peeled tart apples
- ¼ cup sugar
- 2 tsp. plain flour
- 1 tsp. lemon juice
- ¼ tsp. ground cinnamon

Pumpkin Filling

- 1 ½ cups canned pumpkin
- 1 cup fat free evaporated milk
- ½ cup egg substitute
- ½ cup sugar
- ¼ tsp. ground cinnamon

- ¼ tsp. salt
- ⅛ tsp. ground nutmeg

Topping

- ½ cup plain flour
- 3 Tbsp. sugar
- 4 ½ tsp. cold butter
- 3 Tbsp. chopped walnuts

Instructions

1. On a lightly floured surface, unroll pastry.
2. Transfer pastry to a 9- in. deep-dish pie plate.
3. Trim pastry to ½ inch beyond the edge of the plate; flute edges!
4. In a large bowl, combine the apples, sugar, flour, lemon juice and cinnamon. Spoon into crust.
5. In another large bowl, whisk the pumpkin filling ingredients. Pour over apple mixture.
6. Bake at 375 degrees for 30 minutes.
7. For topping, combine flour and sugar.
8. Cut in butter until crumbly, stir in walnuts.
9. Sprinkle over pie.
10. Bake 20-25 minutes longer or until a knife inserted into pumpkin layer comes out clean (cover edges during the last 15 minutes to prevent over browning if necessary).
11. Cool on a wire rack. Refrigerate leftovers.

Recipe type: Desserts - Pies
Serves: 6-8
Prep time: 20 mins
Cook time: 45 mins
Total time: 1 hr 5 mins

CRUNCH TOP PEACH PIE

Ingredients

- ½ cup sugar
- ¼ cup flour
- ¼ tsp. cinnamon
- ½ tsp. salt
- 4 cups sliced peaches, fresh peeled
- 9-inch single pie crust
- 1 tbsp butter

Crunch Topping

- ¾ cup flour
- ½ cup brown sugar
- ½ cup butter softened
- ½ cup chopped walnuts

Instructions

1. Preheat oven to 400 degrees.
2. Combine sugar, flour, cinnamon and salt.
3. Gently stir in peaches to coat and set aside.
4. Spoon peach mixture into pie crust and dot with butter.

5. Combine crunch topping and sprinkle over peach mixture.
6. Bake at 400 degrees for 10 minutes.
7. Reduce heat to 350 degrees and bake for 45 minutes.

Recipe type: Desserts - Pies
Serves: 8
Prep time: 15 mins
Cook time: 55 mins
Total time: 1 hr 10 mins

FRENCH SILK CHOCOLATE PIE

A wonderful, rich French silk chocolate pie that has to be tasted to be believed. Rich and creamy in a way that store-bought pies can never hope to be.

Ingredients

- ¼ cup sugar
- 3 Tbsp. cornstarch
- 1 ½ cup milk
- 1 6 oz. bag semi-sweet chocolate chips
- 1 tsp. vanilla
- ¾ cup heavy cream
- 1 Tbsp. powdered sugar

Instructions

1. In medium saucepan combine sugar and cornstarch.
2. Blend well.
3. Gradually add milk.

4. Cook over medium heat, stirring constantly until mixture boils.
5. Add chocolate chips and vanilla, stirring until chips and melted and mixture is smooth.
6. Pour into large mixing bowl, cover with plastic wrap and cool to room temperature.
7. In large bowl or mixer combine heavy cream and confectioners' sugar.
8. Beat until soft peaks form.
9. Chill for 2 or 3 hours.
10. Beat cooled chocolate mixture at medium speed about 1 minute until light and fluffy.
11. Fold into whipped cream.
12. Spoon into crust.

Recipe type: Desserts - Pies
Serves: 8
Prep time: 3 hrs
Cook time: 15 mins
Total time: 3 hrs 15 mins

MILLION DOLLAR PIE

"This is one of my favorite pies. A lot of folks around these parts are familiar with it also. Try it when you are hungry for something easy, cool and scrumptious."
~ *Mama Peggy*

Ingredients

- 1 can sweetened condensed milk
- Juice of two lemons
- 1 (9 oz.) ctn. cool whip
- 1 cup chopped pecans
- 1 can of crushed pineapple, drained

Instructions

1. Beat lemon juice and milk on low with an electric mixer, for about a minute.
2. Then fold in the cool whip, along with the pineapple and pecans.
3. Pour into a graham cracker crust.
4. Chill for about an hour before serving. Makes two (9-inch) pies.

Recipe type: Desserts - Pies
Serves: 16
Prep time: 20 mins
Cook time: 0 mins
Total time: 20 mins

OLD FASHIONED GOLDEN APPLE PIE

"An old fashioned golden apple pie recipe. If I had to make the choice of what pie I loved better than any, it would be hands down APPLE! You can't beat a warm piece of homemade apple pie with ice cream! Um-Um good!!!"
~ Mama Peggy

Ingredients

- 5 to 7 Golden Delicious apples, about 2 lbs.
- 1 Tbsp. lemon juice
- ⅓ cup sugar
- 1 tsp. sugar
- 1 tsp. cinnamon
- ⅛ tsp. nutmeg
- ¼ tsp. salt
- 2 Tbsp. flour
- pastry for two 9inch pies
- 2 Tbsp. butter or margarine

Instructions

1. Peel, core and slice apples 1/4 -inch thick to equal 7 cups.
2. Sprinkle with lemon juice.
3. Combine sugar, spices, salt and flour.
4. Toss with apples.
5. Place into pastry-lined pie plate.
6. Dot with butter or margarine; adjust top crust.
7. Seal and flute edges; cut vents into top crust.

8. Bake at 400 degrees for 40 to 50 minutes or until crust is golden brown and tender!

Recipe type: Desserts – Pies
Serves: 8-10
Prep time: 20 mins
Cook time: 50 mins
Total time: 1 hr 10 mins

PEANUT BUTTER PIE

The best dessert ever for fans of peanut butter. This rich pie is loved by kids and adults alike! And what's not to love? It's peanut butter!

Ingredients

- 3 eggs
- 1 cup dark corn syrup
- ½ cup granulated sugar
- ½ cup creamy peanut butter
- ½ tsp. vanilla extract
- 1 cup salted peanuts
- 1 unbaked 9-inch pie shell

Instructions

1. Preheat oven to 400 degrees.
2. In a large bowl, beat the eggs along with the corn syrup, peanut butter, and vanilla until nice and smooth.
3. Stir in the peanuts.

4. Pour the filling into the pie shell.
5. Bake for 15 minutes.
6. Reduce oven to 350 degrees and bake the pie for another 30 to 35 minutes until it's golden brown on the top.
7. Allow pie to cool on the rack.

Recipe type: Desserts – Pies
Serves: 8-10
Prep time: 15 mins
Cook time: 50 mins
Total time: 1 hr 5 mins

Pinto Bean Pie

An old-fashioned Southern recipe, from back in the days when you made do with what you had! This pinto bean pie recipe is better than you would think. Try it! You'll like it.

Ingredients

- 1 cup pinto beans, mashed well
- 1 cup shredded coconut
- 1 cup pecans
- 3 cups sugar
- 4 eggs
- 1 tsp. vanilla flavoring
- 1 cup milk
- 1 ½ sticks butter

Instructions

1. Add all of your ingredients together in a large bowl.
2. Mix well!
3. Pour into 3 pie shells.
4. Back for 1 hour at 300 degrees.

Recipe type: Desserts – Pies
Serves: 8-10
Prep time: 12 mins
Cook time: 1 hr
Total time: 1 hr 20 mins

Pumpkin Pie

"An old fashioned golden apple pie recipe. If I had to make the choice of what pie I loved better than any, it would be hands down APPLE! You can't beat a warm piece of homemade apple pie with ice cream! Um-Um good!!!"
~ Mama Peggy

Ingredients

- 1 9-inch unbaked piecrust
- 3 eggs, separated
- 1 16 oz. can pumpkin (2 cups)
- 1 cup evaporated milk
- 1 cup sugar
- 1 tsp. ground cinnamon
- ½ tsp. ground ginger
- ¼ tsp. ground nutmeg
- ¼ tsp. salt

Instructions

1. Prepare unbaked pie crust.
2. Preheat oven to 375.
3. In a small bowl with mixer at high speed, beat egg whites until soft peaks form.
4. In a large with the same beaters and with mixer at low speed, beat together egg yolks, pumpkin and the rest of the ingredients until well blended.
5. With wire whisk or a rubber spatula, gently fold beaten egg whites into the pumpkin mixture.
6. Pour filling into your crust.

7. Bake 45 minutes until filling is set and a knife inserted 1 inch from the edge comes out clean.
8. Refrigerate until ready to serve.

Recipe type: Desserts – Pies
Serves: 8-10
Prep time: 15 mins
Cook time: 45 mins
Total time: 1 hr

Ritz Cracker Pecan Pie

Ingredients

- 20 Ritz crackers – crumbled
- 3 egg whites, beaten
- 1 cup pecans, chopped
- 1 cup sugar
- 1 tsp. vanilla
- 1 cup whipping cream, whipped

Instructions

5. Mix all ingredients and bake in a buttered 9-inch pan, no crust, for 25 minutes at 350 degrees.
6. Top with whipped cream.
7. Refrigerate 2 or more hours before serving.
8. Serves 6.

Recipe type: Desserts – Pies
Serves: 8-10
Prep time: 10 mins
Cook time: 25 mins
Total time: 35 mins

STRAWBERRY PIE

Ingredients

- 1 ½ cups sugar
- ¼ cup cornstarch
- ¼ tsp. salt
- 2 cups sugar
- 1 (3 oz.) Strawberry gelatin
- 3 cups strawberries
- 1 pie shell, baked
- 1 container Cool Whip

Instructions

1. Bring to boil; sugar, cornstarch, salt and water.
2. Add strawberry gelatin, stir well.
3. Let cool.
4. Add strawberries to baked pie shell.
5. Cover with whipped cream or Cool whip!

"This recipe has been around for ages but you can't get tired if it! It's simply delicious! If by chance you have never tried it (especially with fresh berries straight out of the field) then you must try it! You will never regret it, I promise you!!!!!" ~ *Mama Peggy*

Recipe type: Desserts – Pies
Serves: 8-10
Prep time: 25 mins
Cook time: 15 mins
Total time: 40 mins

Sweet Potato Pie

"This is simpler version of sweet potato pie but it is good too! I'm certainly looking forward to Thanksgiving! It's my favorite time of the year. A time to stop and reflect on how much we have to be thankful for! I hope God has been as good to you as He has been to me!"

~ *Mama Peggy, Oct. 21, 2010*

Ingredients

- 1 ⅓ cups pie crust mix
- ¼ cup chopped pecans
- 3 to 4 Tbsp. cold water
- 3 eggs
- 2 cans (15 oz. each) sweet potatoes, drained
- 1 can (14 oz.) sweetened condensed milk
- 1 ½ to 2 tsp. pumpkin pie spice
- 1 tsp. vanilla extract
- ½ tsp. salt
- Whipped topping and additional chopped pecans (optional)

Instructions

1. In a small bowl, combine pie crust mix and pecans.
2. Gradually add water, tossing with a fork until dough forms a ball.
3. Roll out to fit a 9-inch deep dish pie plate. Transfer pastry to pie plate. Flute edges; set aside.
4. In a food processor, combine the eggs, sweet potatoes, milk, pumpkin pie spice, vanilla and salt; blend until smooth. Pour into pastry.
5. Bake at 425 degrees for 15 minutes.
6. Reduce heat to 350 degrees, bake 30 to 35 minutes longer or until or until a knife inserted near the center comes out clean.
7. Cool on a wire rack.
8. Garnish with whipped cream and toasted pecans if you like! Enjoy! My mouth is watering already!

Editor's Note: We have used frozen pie crusts with this recipe, and received no complaints. If you don't feel like wrangling with making your own crust, a frozen crust is a handy alternative.

Recipe type: Desserts – Pies
Serves: 8-10
Prep time: 20 mins
Cook time: 50 mins
Total time: 1 hr 10 mins

TERESA'S CREAM PIE

"A recipe from my niece, Teresa Hicks." ~ *Mama Peggy*

Ingredients

- 1 (8 oz.) pkg. cream cheese
- 8 oz. sour cream
- ½ cup sugar

Instructions

1. Blend together cream cheese, sour cream and fold in 3 cups Cool Whip. Then spoon into a graham cracker crusts and top with any kind fruit… blueberries, strawberries or peaches etc.
2. Garnish with whipped cream and toasted pecans if you like! Enjoy! My mouth is watering already!
3. Makes two pies.

Recipe type: Desserts – Pies
Serves: 8-10
Prep time: 20 mins
Cook time: 0 mins
Total time: 20 mins

Wonderful Lemon Pie

"Once you make this, you will find it will be the only lemon pie recipe you will ever need. I guarantee!!!"

~ *Mama Peggy*

Ingredients

- 1 cup sugar
- 3 Tbsp. cornstarch
- 1 cup milk
- ¼ cup butter
- ¼ cup lemon juice
- 3 egg yolks, slightly beaten
- 1 cup sour cream
- 1 9-inch baked pie shell

Instructions

1. Combine sugar, cornstarch, butter, lemon juice, milk and egg yolks in heavy saucepan.
2. Cook over medium heat, stirring constantly, until smooth and thickened.
3. Remove from heat, cover with wax paper and cool.
4. When cool, fold sour cream into mixture and pour into baked pie shell.
5. Chill at least two hours.
6. Top with cool whip.

Recipe type: Desserts – Pies
Serves: 8-10
Prep time: 2 hrs 15 mins
Cook time: 0 mins
Total time: 2 hrs 15 mins

Peggy's Blog – Woodpecker!
January 18, 2009

The funniest thing happened to me this morning! My friend Libby is an avid bird lover and has a bird feeder on her window. I was at her apartment this morning and a lot of different kinds of birds were flying around the feeder trying to fight to get their portion. All at once, Bump!, one bird flew into the window pane. We both jumped, and I said "Oh! goodness. I'll bet that little bird got hurt." I looked toward the small tree nearby and saw a bird just shaking its head. It looked kinda odd to me because I had never seen a bird do that. I told Libby to look at that bird, it had to be the one that hit the window, because of the way it was shaking its little head. Libby looked and started laughing! Then she said "Peggy, that's a woodpecker".

That was the first woodpecker I had ever seen, in all my 76years (Will be in May!). I asked her "Can he really peck holes in that branch?" She said yes, still laughing at me. Loretta loved birds as much as Libby does. She would go out into the backyard, after we came home from the cafe every afternoon and feed those birds. Sometimes when we got home, on the telephone lines across our property, birds would be sitting from one end to the other, waiting on her to feed them. We would get the biggest kick out of that!

I have learned all about birds from watching from Libby's window. She tells me which each one is which. We saw about five big fat robins one day last week. You name it! We've seen it.

Libby and I share something special. We laugh at one another's silly jokes and also the crazy things older folks do.

Today she called for me to come over and she had me an Easter coffee cup. It is beautiful and she has one just like it. She said "Now, we have one just alike!" I told her every time I looked at it, I would think of her! She said, "I will think of you too, when I look at mine."

She is failing, now, from all that morphine she has to take, but she will never give up until she absolutely has to. She has taught me so much about hanging in when you have a terminal illness. She cries sometimes! She is human, just as we all are. She shared with the Hospice Chaplain, Dave, yesterday that she wanted to go home to be with her Lord and Savior but also to see her Mom and the rest of her friends and family. She has really fought a battle but I think she is getting tired now!

She looked over at me, yesterday, and said "Peggy, I know it hurts you to hear me say this, but this is no way to have to live!" I agree! Yes, my asthma is under control, but I haven't forgotten the dashes to the emergency room, when I would be fighting for my breath. It's a horrible feeling! I've seen her when she had to fight and she's still doing it. Not as often, with all the medicine and morphine she has to take.

My Prayer has been for awhile now, that God won't let her smother to death, that He would just reach down and pick her up in those strong loving arms of His and take her home as she is sleeping.

When she wakes, the first face she will see is Jesus, Her Lord. Then she will see Rudy, Her husband. What a wonderful, glorious day, that will be.

Desserts – Pudding & Other

Cherry Supreme Dessert

"This is an easy dish to prepare! Especially for you working mom's. Enjoy!" ~ *Mama Peggy*

Ingredients

- ¾ cup rice cereal
- ¼ cup chopped walnuts
- 2 Tbsp. brown sugar
- 2 Tbsp. butter, melted
- 4 cups miniature marshmallows
- 1 cup heavy whipping cream, whipped
- 1 can (21 oz.) cherry pie filling

Instructions

1. In a small bowl, combine the cereal, walnuts, brown sugar and butter.
2. Press into a greased 8-inch square dish.
3. Fold marshmallows into whipped cream.
4. Spread over cereal mixture.
5. Top with pie filling.
6. Cover and refrigerate for at least two hours!

"It would be even quicker if you use Cool Whip! That's what I do sometimes!" ~ *Mama Peggy*

Recipe type: Desserts - Pudding & Other
Serves: 8
Prep time: 20 mins
Cook time: 10 mins
Total time: 30 mins

GINGERBREAD PUMPKIN TRIFLE

Ingredients

- ½ cup shortening
- ⅓ cup sugar
- 1 cup molasses
- 1 egg
- 2 ⅓ cups all-purpose flour
- 1 tsp. baking soda
- 1 tsp. ground ginger
- 1 tsp. ground cinnamon
- ¾ tsp. salt
- ¾ cup hot water

Filling/Topping

- 2 cups cold milk
- 1 package (3.4 oz.) instant vanilla pudding mix
- 1 can (15 oz.) solid pack pumpkin
- ½ cup packed brown sugar
- 1 tsp. vanilla extract
- ½ tsp. ground cinnamon
- 2 cups heavy whipping cream
- ⅓ cup sugar
- 1 tsp. rum extract

Instructions

1. In a large bowl, cream shortening and sugar until light and fluffy.
2. Beat in molasses and egg.
3. Combine flour, baking soda, ginger, cinnamon and salt; add to creamed mixture alternately with water, beating well after each addition.
4. Pour into greased 13 x 9-inch baking pan.
5. Bake at 350 degrees for 25-30 minutes or until a toothpick inserted near the center comes out clean.
6. Cool on a wire rack.
7. Cut the gingerbread into ½- to 1-inch cubes, and set aside.
8. In a large bowl, whisk milk and pudding mix for 2 minutes. Let stand for 2 minutes or until soft-set.
9. Combine the pumpkin, brown sugar, vanilla and cinnamon; stir into pudding.
10. In another bowl, beat cream until it begins to thicken.
11. Add sugar and extract; beat until stiff peaks form.
12. Set aside ¼ cup gingerbread cubes.
13. In a 4-quart. glass serving bowl, layer a third of the remaining gingerbread cubes, top with a third of the pumpkin mixture and whipped cream.
14. Repeat layers twice.
15. Crumble reserved gingerbread, sprinkle over top.
16. Cover and refrigerate for at least an hour before serving!

"This would be a wonderful dessert for Thanksgiving! I love gingerbread just by itself alone but it is awesome mixed with all these other ingredients!!! ENJOY!!!!"
~ *Mama Peggy*

Recipe type: Desserts - Pudding & Other
Serves: 8
Prep time: 45 mins
Cook time: 30 mins
Total time: 1 hr 15 mins

COCONUT RICE PUDDING

Ingredients

- 2 ¾ cups water
- ¾ cup long grain rice
- 1 can (15 oz.) cream of coconut (not coconut milk)
- 1 can (12 oz.) evaporated milk
- ⅔ cup sweetened flaked coconut (optional)
- 1 Tbsp. dark Rum (optional) - or I would probably use rum flavoring

Instructions

1. In a 4 ½ to 6-quart slow cooker bowl, stir water, rice, cream of coconut, and evaporated milk until combined.
2. Cover slow cooker with lid and cook as on low setting 4 to 5 hours, or high setting 2 ½ to 3 hours.
3. If you like, while pudding is cooking, toast coconut: Heat nonstick small skillet over medium heat until

hot. Add coconut; cook 4 to 5 minutes or until lightly browned, stirring constantly. Transfer coconut to plate.
4. Remove bowl from slow cooker.
5. Stir in rum (or rum flavoring), if using.
6. Let the pudding stand 10 minutes.
7. Transfer to serving bowl.
8. If you won't be serving right away, press sheet of plastic wrap onto pudding; refrigerate up to 2 days.
9. To serve, spoon pudding into dessert bowls and sprinkle with toasted coconut if using.

Recipe type: Desserts - Pudding & Other
Serves: 8
Prep time: 20 mins
Cook time: 5 hrs
Total time: 5 hrs 20 mins

HOMEMADE VANILLA PUDDING

Store-bought vanilla pudding, whether in a mix or pre-made, just can't hold a candle to real, homemade vanilla pudding. What wonderful memories one must have if they remember their mother or grandmother making fresh, homemade vanilla pudding in the kitchen. A yummy treat that will never go out of style!

Ingredients

- 3 cups of 2% milk
- 1 Tbsp. vanilla
- 6 large egg yolks

- ¾ cup sugar
- 4 Tbsp. corn starch
- Pinch of salt
- Sliced banana (optional)
- Gingersnap cookies (optional)

Instructions

1. Heat milk and vanilla in a deep pot on medium heat.
2. While that's slowly warming, combine sugar, corn starch and salt in a mixing bowl.
3. Add the egg yolks to the corn starch and sugar mixture and whisk it really well.
4. When the milk just starts to simmer, gradually add about half of it to the cornstarch and sugar mixture (be sure to whisk it the whole time to temper the eggs).
5. Pour that mixture back into the hot milk and cook it over medium heat, stirring constantly, until it starts to bubble and thicken.
6. Take it off the heat and pour it into a large, shallow pan or baking dish, and cover the top tightly with plastic wrap.
7. Make sure the plastic wrap is covering the surface of the pudding and poke it all over with a sharp knife to help let the heat escape.
8. Pop it in the fridge for 2 or 3 hours so it has a chance to cool down and set up.
9. Serve it (one way) combined with banana slices in a wine glass, topped with a couple gingersnap cookies.

Recipe type: Desserts – Pudding & Other
Serves: 8
Prep time: 15 mins
Cook time: 15 mins
Total time: 30 mins

Ice Cream Cake

"This is to die for!!!!!!!" ~ Mama Peggy

Ingredients

- 1 lg. box of 24 ice cream sandwiches (Pet is best)
- 2 (12 oz.) containers of Cool Whip or equivalent
- 1 large bottle of Chocolate fudge topping
- 1 cup pecans and/or favorite fruit (optional)

Instructions

1. Place one layer of sandwiches in a 9 x 12-inch Pyrex dish, cover with Cool Whip.
2. Place another layer of sandwiches in pan, cover with Cool Whip again.
3. Make a garnish of strawberries or other fruits pecans or combination.
4. Squirt ice cream topping in a pattern over the dessert.
5. Place in freezer until ready to serve.

Recipe type: Desserts – Pudding & Other
Serves: 6-8
Prep time: 20 mins
Cook time: 0 mins
Total time: 20 mins

LUCILLE'S CHRISTMAS ICEBOX FRUIT CAKE

"This is a very old recipe. I think that the marshmallow cream that is used in making fudge would work, as well."
~ *Mama Peggy*

Ingredients

- 1 box Spice cake mix (Bake as directed)
- ½ cup Candied green cherries
- ½ cup Candied red cherries
- 4 cups mixed fruit
- 1 pkg. (8 oz.) chopped dates
- 2 ½ cups raisins
- 4 ½ cups chopped pecans
- Pkg. fluffy white icing mix (Betty Crocker) Mix as directed.

Instructions

1. Crumble cake into fruit and nut mixture.
2. Add icing.
3. Mix.
4. Pack into loaf pans and refrigerate.

5. This is a very old recipe. I think the marshmallow cream that is used in making fudge would work, as well.

Recipe type: Desserts – Pudding & Other
Serves: 6-8
Prep time: 15 mins
Cook time: 0 mins
Total time: 15 mins

MAPLE WALNUT STICKY BUNS

Ingredients

- 1 cup milk plus 2 Tbsp.
- 2 pkgs. (1 -1/2 tbsp) active dry yeast
- ⅔ cup granulated sugar
- 21 tbsp unsalted butter, softened
- 3 eggs, at room temperature
- 5 ⅓ cups all-purpose flour
- 1 ¼ tsp. salt
- 3 tsp. maple extract
- 1 cup packed light brown sugar
- 2 cups walnuts, chopped
- ⅓ cup caramel topping (Smucker's)
- 1 ½ cups confectioners' sugar

Instructions

1. Scald 1 cup milk (heat to steaming).
2. In a mixing bowl combine warm milk, yeast and sugar.

3. Let yeast start to bubble, about 5 minutes.
4. Add 12 Tbsp. butter and eggs to mixer and beat, with the paddle attachment, until slightly blended.
5. Stir in flour and salt, about 2 minutes.
6. Scrape down sides of bowl and continue mixing on medium speed to develop the dough. 3 minutes more
7. Transfer dough to a greased bowl and cover with plastic wrap; set aside in a warm place and let rise until doubled, about an hour.
8. Grease two large- up muffin tins.
9. Melt 6 Tbsp. butter and stir in 1 ½ tsp. maple extract; set aside.
10. Gently punch down dough and divide in half. Roll into 2 ½ by 18-inch rectangles on a lightly floured work surface.
11. Spread maple-butter mixture evenly over both rectangles.
12. Sprinkle each with half the brown sugar and walnuts.
13. Roll tightly into logs, starting at the long edge and pinch seams together.
14. Cut each log into 6 3-inche pieces for a total of 12 buns.
15. Place in muffin tins cut side up.
16. Cover and allow to rise for 30 minutes.
17. Heat oven to 325 degrees. Bake until golden brown, 28 to 30 minutes.
18. Combine caramel topping and 1½ tsp. of maple extract.
19. Carefully remove hot buns from pan and place on a clean baking sheet; drizzle with caramel.

Recipe type: Desserts – Pudding & Other
Serves: 12
Prep time: 55 mins
Cook time: 30 mins
Total time: 1 hr 25 mins

MY MAMA'S BREAD PUDDING

Ingredients

- 4 or 5 soft cold biscuits
- 2 cups milk
- ½ cup butter
- 1 cup sugar
- ½ tsp. cinnamon
- ¼ tsp. salt
- 2 eggs (beaten)
- ½ cup raisins (if desired)
- 1 tsp. vanilla

Instructions

1. Pour milk over crumbled biscuits.
2. After a few minutes add other ingredients except butter.
3. Mix well and pour into 1 ½-quart casserole dish!
4. Dot with butter.
5. Bake at 350 degrees for 40 to 45 minutes!

"We were raised eating bread pudding. You can experiment as I do! Sometimes I add cocoa instead of cinnamon and raisins and I have chocolate bread pudding! Taste to make sure you don't need more sugar. Some people like it better with a little bit more! Enjoy!" ~ *Mama Peggy*

[Editor's Note: I don't remember Mama ever making her bread pudding with cinnamon and raisins. When she made it for us, or at the café, it was always with cocoa, and it was always amazing. The end result was nothing like one expects when they mention "bread pudding". It's in a class all its own.]

Recipe type: Desserts – Pudding & Other
Serves: 10-12
Prep time: 15 mins
Cook time: 45 mins
Total time: 1 hr

NEVER FAIL MERINGUE

"I must admit that for some reason, as old as I am now, I have always had a little trouble with my meringues. That is until I found this little jewel and I have used it for a long time now. It really works and very well I might add!" ~ *Mama Peggy, Sept. 3, 2009*

Ingredients

- 1 Tbsp. cornstarch
- ½ cup boiling water
- 2 Tbsp. cold water
- 3 egg whites
- 6 Tbsp. sugar
- pinch of salt

- 1 tsp. vanilla

Instructions

1. Blend cornstarch and cold water in saucepan.
2. Add boiling water and cook, stirring until clear and thick.
3. Let stand until completely cold.
4. With electric beater at high speed, beat egg whites until foamy.
5. Gradually add sugar and beat until stiff but not dry.
6. Turn mixer to low and add salt and vanilla.
7. Gradually beat in cold cornstarch mixture.
8. Turn mixer again on high and beat well.
9. Spread meringue over cooled pie filling.
10. Bake at 350 degrees for about 10 minutes.

"You gotta try this meringue, folks. It cuts beautifully and never gets sticky!" ~ *Mama Peggy*

Recipe type: Desserts – Pudding & Other
Serves: 1 pie
Prep time: 15 mins
Cook time: 10 mins
Total time: 25 mins

OLD FASHIONED SNOW CREAM

Ingredients

- 4 cups fresh snow
- 1 cup cream or milk
- ¾ cup sugar
- 1 tsp. vanilla extract

Instructions

1. Place snow into a large bowl.
2. Pour milk over the snow and add vanilla.
3. Mix to combine.
4. Serve immediately in bowls.
5. NOTE: In place of sugar and milk, you can substitute ½ cup of sweetened condensed milk.

Recipe type: Desserts – Pudding & Other
Serves: 4
Prep time: 5 mins
Cook time: 5 mins
Total time: 10 mins

Orange Fluff Salad

"I ran across this salad a while back and I love to try recipes of this kind! Switch the ingredients around a bit, and try it different ways! Like a different kind of jello and a different fruit! I believe it will be one of your favorite salads on Holidays! Simple but Delicious!" ~ *Mama Peggy*

Ingredients

- 8 oz. Cool Whip
- 8 oz. sour cream
- 1 (3 oz.) box orange Jell-O
- 2 cups miniature Marshmallows
- 2 cups Mandarin oranges (drained)

Instructions

1. Mix cool whip, sour cream and Jello together.
2. Fold in Marshmallows and Oranges.
3. Then chill.
4. Enjoy!!

Recipe type: Desserts – Pudding & Other
Serves: 8
Prep time: 10 mins
Cook time: 10 mins
Total time: 20 mins

PEGGY'S APPLE CRUMBLE PIE COBBLER

"My Friend Libby and her son Warren made a trip to an apple orchard located near Asheville, N.C. They allow you to pick your own apples. I wasn't able to go so they brought me a peck of the biggest, most beautiful apples you have ever seen. This recipe is what I came up with for some of those apples. I hope you like it. I sure did! The only thing wrong was I didn't have ice cream on hand to go with it!!!" ~ *Mama Peggy*

Ingredients

- 2 (9-inch) pie shells, thawed
- 10 cups thinly sliced apples
- 2 Tbsp. lemon juice (optional)
- 1 ½ cups white sugar
- 4 Tbsp. all-purpose flour
- 1 tsp. ground cinnamon
- 1 tsp. ground nutmeg
- 1 cup chopped pecans
- 1 cup all-purpose flour 1 cup brown sugar
- 1 stick margarine or butter
- 1 cup raisins (optional)

Instructions

1. Preheat oven to 375 degrees F.
2. Place sliced apples in a large bowl. Sprinkle with juice if you prefer.
3. In a small bowl, mix together white sugar, 4 Tbsp. flour, cinnamon and nutmeg.

4. Sprinkle mixture over apples.
5. Toss until apples are evenly coated.
6. Stir in pecans (and raisins if desired).
7. Place thawed pie crusts in 9-x 15-inch pan that has been sprayed with Pam.
8. Shape crusts with fingers to fit bottom of pan and a little up the sides.
9. Spoon apple mixture into crust.
10. In a small bowl mix together, 1 cup flour, and 1 cup brown sugar.
11. Cut in butter or margarine until mixture is crumbly.
12. Sprinkle mixture over apple filling.
13. Cover loosely with aluminum foil.
14. Bake in preheated oven for 30 minutes.
15. Remove foil and bake an additional 25 to 30 minutes or until golden brown.

Recipe type: Desserts – Pudding & Other
Serves: 10
Prep time: 20 mins
Cook time: 60 mins
Total time: 1 hr 20 mins

PEGGY'S BANANA PUDDING

"When I made banana pudding at Peggy's restaurant, it took twelve lbs. of bananas and about 6 boxes of vanilla wafers. Every dish was made from 'scratch' as we Southerners called it. Banana pudding was one of our best sellers. ENJOY!" ~ *Mama Peggy*

Ingredients

- 3 egg yolks + 1 whole egg
- 3 egg whites
- 1 cup sugar
- 1 Tbsp. flour(plain)
- 1 (11 oz.) box vanilla wafers
- 3 Tbsp. sugar
- 1 cup sweet milk
- 1 cup evaporated milk
- pinch of salt
- 1 tsp. vanilla
- 3 large ripe bananas
- 1 tsp. rum flavoring

Instructions

1. Place in mixer bowl the egg yolks, plus 1 egg, 1 cup sugar, flour, and salt. Beat this until creamy and yellow color.
2. Add sweet milk, canned milk, vanilla and rum flavorings.
3. Pour into saucepan on medium heat and let come to boiling point, stirring constantly. Do not boil.

4. Remove from heat.
5. In Pyrex dish, layer vanilla wafers, next layer of bananas, sliced thin. Repeat until wafers and bananas are gone.
6. Next pour custard mix all over and let seep down through bananas and wafers.
7. Beat egg whites stiff.
8. Add 3 Tbsp. sugar and ½ tsp. vanilla.
9. Place on top of pudding mixture and bake for 10 or 15 minutes at 350 degrees or enough to brown meringue.

Recipe type: Desserts – Pudding & Other
Serves: 10
Prep time: 15 mins
Cook time: 15 mins
Total time: 30 mins

RUNNING TOWARDS CHOCOLATE

One of the last conversations we had with Mama Peggy was when she called to tell us she had filled out a survey online and found out that her "Indian name" was "Running Towards Chocolate". This recipe, which we've seen called "Santa's Suicide" and "Slutty Brownies" is just the sort of dessert Mama Peggy loved. It's the ultimate chocolate chip cookie, Oreo and fudge brownie bar.

Ingredients

- 1 (16.5 oz) pkg. Pillsbury Chocolate Chip cookie dough
- 1 Family Side pkg. Oreo Double Stuff cookies
- 1 pkg. Duncan Hines Double Fudge brownie mix
- ice cream
- Hershey's chocolate syrup

Instructions

1. Line a 9 x 13-inch baking dish with parchment paper and spray with cooking spray. You don't have to, but it's easier to get them out this way.
2. Line bottom of dish with cookie dough, making sure to cover the bottom evenly.
3. Cover the cookie dough with a layer of Oreo cookies.
4. Mix up your brownie batter according to direction and spread over top of the mixture.
5. Bake in oven at 350 degrees for 45-55 minutes.
6. Serve as-is, or topped with a little ice cream and chocolate syrup. How decadent do you want to be?

Recipe type: Desserts – Pudding & Other
Serves: 10
Prep time: 15 mins
Cook time: 55 mins
Total time: 1 hr 10 mins

STRAWBERRY COBBLER

"I just took one of these cobblers out of the oven. The oooh's and aaah's was music to my ears!"

~ *Mama Peggy, Sept. 3 2009*

Ingredients

- 2 pints fresh strawberries (or frozen)
- 2 cups sugar
- 2 Tbsp. cornstarch

Instructions

1. Mix cornstarch and sugar together thoroughly and stir into strawberries.
2. Place over medium heat in heavy saucepan and cook until this thickens.
3. Set aside and make the following crust.

Batter:

- 1 stick of margarine or butter (melted)
- 1 cup of self-rising flour
- ½ cup of water mixed with ½ cup evaporated milk
- 1 tsp. vanilla flavoring
- ¾ cup sugar

Instructions

1. Pour the strawberry mixture into a 9 x 15-inch baking pan that has been sprayed with Pam.
2. Mix all ingredients of batter and slowly pour over the strawberries.
3. Bake at 425 degrees for about 30 minutes, or until the crust browns.
4. Test to see if it's done in the middle.

Recipe type: Desserts – Pudding & Other
Serves: 12-14
Prep time: 30 mins
Cook time: 30 mins
Total time: 1 hr

STRAWBERRY FRUIT SALAD

Ingredients

- 1 small can crushed pineapple
- 1 (3 oz.) box Strawberry gelatin
- 1 lb. Strawberries, sliced
- 3 Bananas, mashed

Instructions

1. Drain juice from pineapple, add enough water to juice to equal two cups liquid.
2. Bring to boil, dissolve gelatin in liquid.
3. Add 1 cup cold water.
4. Cool until thickened.

5. Add strawberries, pineapple and bananas.
6. Pour into 9 x 13-inch pan.
7. Chill until set!

Recipe type: Desserts – Pudding & Other
Serves: 8
Prep time: 15 mins
Cook time: 15 mins
Total time: 30 mins

Strawberry Pudding

Ingredients

- 2 cups fresh Strawberries (sliced)
- 1 (3. oz) box strawberry gelatin
- 2 boxes instant Vanilla Pudding
- 2 cups milk
- 1 small carton sour cream
- 1 box of Vanilla wafers
- 1 (8 oz.) container Cool Whip (any other kind can be used)

Instructions

1. Mix strawberries and gelatin (don't use water) in saucepan.
2. Heat until gelatin dissolves, then set it aside.
3. Mix pudding and milk until it becomes thick, then stir in sour cream and Cool Whip. Mix well.
4. Alternate layers in this order: Wafers, strawberry mixture, and pudding.

5. Chill 3 to 4 hours before serving.

Recipe type: Desserts – Pudding & Other
Serves: 8
Prep time: 15 mins
Cook time: 15 mins
Total time: 30 mins

Peggy's Blog – Sunshine and Warm Weather
May 8, 2009

What two wonderful days we have had this weekend. Last weekend we were covered with a blanket of snow! The snow was just absolutely beautiful, but cold on the bones of all the seniors here at our senior complex. Nothing was stirring, not even a mouse! We just could not stay away from the windows though. One lady said she turned out all her lights, curled up on the couch, and looked out the window as snow fell, lit up by the security lights. What is that saying, "Once a man, twice a child"?

The temperature reached nearly 80 degrees both yesterday and today. It sure lifted my spirits a lot. Libby and I rode to Tony's, in Gastonia, yesterday and got a Banana split each. My, Oh My! I needed that like I needed a hole in my head. If you haven't been fortunate enough to have an ice cream place like Tony's near where you live, you have missed something wonderful (but fattening). We won't even go there!!!

Lately I have been thinking about how I drop in on Victoria and Kevin everyday (via phone calls). They tell me they don't mind but I'm sure they must. I remember when I was married to Jim, that every time his folks would drop by to see us, just as soon as they would leave he would say, "Well, wonder what they were trying to find out this time", or something of that sort!

Bob's mother put me through some hard times because she was so jealous of me, because he married me. But I have to say, I think she loved me like a daughter before she died. So did Jim's mother. After our marriage broke up, every time she came into the restaurant to eat, when I walked over to speak to her, tears would roll down her cheeks.

I guess all of that sort of "marked me" as my mama used to say. I am so afraid of stepping out of my place, that I am always questioning them about it! Kevin is my only child, but he is certainly NOT a mama's boy, Thank God. He loves me, as every child should love their mother, and he has always looked out for me. I have always prayed, from day one, that he would find a girl who would love him as much as he deserved to be loved, and that he would love her in the exact same way. Well , my Prayers were answered when God brought Victoria into his life again. They are like two peas in a pod and I have never seen him happier than he is right now. I just don't want to ever do anything that would make her think that I was trying to hold on to him. I couldn't be happier than I am now. Because Kevin has finally found his soul mate. I believe that with all my heart and I give God the credit for it all. The only thing! I wish He would have brought them together years earlier, so I could hear the pitter-patter of little feet running through my house.

Victoria has two beautiful grown daughters, though, that I will gladly accept as my granddaughters if they will but accept me. God knows what He is doing. He knew as old as I was, I would rather have two already grown grands (as my friends of color calls their grandchildren).

It's kind of a lonely life when you start going down the other side of the hill! My biggest fear is that I might be a bother to someone or that I might lose my independence. I have a little plaque that reads "Live, so that when you are gone, it will have mattered that you were here".

That's how I want my new family to think of me!

Side Dishes

Traditionally, a side dish is a food item that accompanies the entree or main course at a meal. But there's no law that says you can't make a meal out of these yummy side dishes. Rustle up some cornbread and a glass of sweet Southern tea and you pretty much have everything you need.

Fried Okra

No proper Southern upbringing is complete without Fried Okra. It's easy to make, and fried okra makes a wonderful side dish to just about any meal.

Ingredients

- 2 lbs. okra, sliced
- ¾ cup corn meal
- ½ cup all-purpose flour
- ½ tsp. salt
- ¼ cup Canola or vegetable oil
- ½ cup buttermilk

Instructions

1. Mix together corn meal, flour, and salt in a large mixing bowl.
2. Slicing okra for cooking, and make sure to discard the stem ends and the tips. They're too tough for frying.
3. While you're slicing the okra, heat oil in a large skillet over medium heat. You'll know it's ready when a drop of water added to the oil will sizzle.
4. In a small bowl, drop your sliced okra into the buttermilk (this give your coating something to stick to), and then into your corn meal / flour mixture.

5. Add okra to skillet once well coated and allow to brown on one side, about 3 minutes, before stirring.
6. Once both sides of okra have browned, about 3 more minutes, reduce heat and cook until fork tender (about 10 minutes).

Recipe type: Side Dishes
Serves: 6
Prep time: 15 mins
Cook time: 20 mins
Total time: 35 mins

HUSH PUPPIES

Folks in the Carolinas love their hush puppies. You can find hush puppies in other states, but they're just not the same. Carolina hush puppies are as unique as Carolina barbecue. And just as habit forming!

Ingredients

- 2 cups cornmeal
- 2 Tbsp. flour
- 1 tsp. soda
- 1 tsp. salt
- 1 tsp. baking powder
- 6 Tbsp. chopped onion
- 1 egg
- 2 cups buttermilk

Instructions

7. Beat all of the ingredients together.

1. Either shape into 2 to 3 inch "logs" (Carolina style), or for a round shape use a Tbsp., then drop into hot deep fat fryer (they will float when done).
2. Drain on paper.

Recipe type: Side Dishes
Serves: 8
Prep time: 15 mins
Cook time: 20 mins
Total time: 35 mins

ITALIAN POTATO SALAD

Ingredients

- 3 lbs. potatoes
- ⅓ cup Italian dressing
- 4 hard cooked eggs, chopped
- ¾ cup chopped celery
- ⅓ cup chopped onion
- ¼ cup chopped cucumber
- ¼ cup chopped green pepper
- ½ cup mayonnaise
- ¼ cup sour cream
- 1 tsp. prepared horseradish
- Chopped fresh tomatoes

Instructions

1. Place potatoes in a saucepan; cover with water. Bring to a boil and cook until tender; drain and cool.
2. Peel and cube potatoes; place in large bowl.
3. Add dressing and toss to coat.
4. Cover and chill for 2 hours.
5. Add eggs, celery, onion, cucumber and green pepper. Mix well.
6. In a small bowl, combine mayonnaise, Sour cream and horseradish; mix well.
7. Pour over potato mixture and toss to coat.
8. Chill for at least 1 hour.
9. Top with tomatoes.

Recipe type: Side Dishes
Serves: 8-10
Prep time: 25 mins
Cook time: 45 mins
Total time: 1 hr 10 mins

Low Carb Baked Veggie Cheese Squares

Ingredients

- 2 cups small broccoli florets, or chopped broccoli stems and florets
- 2 cups chopped asparagus stalks
- 2 cups chopped fresh spinach
- 2 cloves garlic
- 1 medium onion, chopped
- 4-5 Tbsp. of flax seeds (optional, but yummy and super healthy!)
- 3 eggs, beaten into submission
- 5 oz. mayo
- 5 oz. sour cream
- 1 cup Parmesan cheese
- 6 oz. sharp cheddar cheese, shredded
- 1 cup carb quik
- ¾ cup panko bread crumbs
- 2 Tbsp. olive oil
- 2 tsp. cayenne pepper
- Salt and Pepper

Instructions

10. Preheat oven to 350
11. In small skillet sauté onions and garlic in olive oil until translucent.
12. Combine all veggies in a large mixing bowl.
13. In small bowl, combine eggs, cheese, mayo and sour cream.
14. Add to veggies.

15. Fold in onions and garlic.
16. Add seasonings.
17. Finally add bread crumbs and carbquik, flax seeds (optional).
18. Mix all together until well blended (if the mix is too dry, you can always add another egg).
19. Press into a 9 x 11-inch casserole pan.
20. Bake at 350 until browned on top, about 45 - 50 minutes.
21. Allow to cool and set up. Cut into squares.

Recipe courtesy of Victoria Sadler Lovelace.

Recipe type: Side Dishes
Serves: 16
Prep time: 10 mins
Cook time: 50 mins
Total time: 1 hr

Old Fashioned Baked Beans

This baked bean recipe is more work than some others, but the first time you taste slow-cooked baked beans, you'll agree they're worth the trouble.

Ingredients

- 3 cups dried Navy beans (about 1½ lbs.)
- ¾ lb. salt pork
- 1 medium onion
- ¼ cup light brown sugar
- 2 tsp. salt
- 2 tsp. dry mustard
- 1 cup light molasses

Instructions

1. Wash the beans the day before, discarding those that just won't do. Cover the beans with 2 quarts of cold water, cover, and refrigerate overnight.
2. The following day, drain the beans and place them in a 6 quart kettle.
3. Cover with 2 quarts of cold water.
4. Bring to a boil, and reduce heat.
5. Simmer, covered, for about 30 minutes.
6. Drain (but keep the liquid).
7. Preheat oven to 300 degrees.
8. Trim the rind from the salt pork and cut the pork almost all the way through at ½-inch spacing.
9. Place the onion in the bottom of a 4 quart bean pot or casserole dish.

10. Add the beans, and bury the pork, with the cut side down, into the center of the beans.
11. Heat that been liquid which you saved to boiling.
12. Combine the rest of the ingredients and pour in 1 cup of the boiling bean liquid to blend ingredients.
13. Pour the mixture over the beans.
14. Add about 1½ cups of boiling liquid, just enough to cover the beans.
15. Baked, covered, for 6 hours, stirring every hour or so to help the beans cook evenly.
16. If beans seem dry after stirring, just add a little boiling water.
17. If you like the top of the beans to brown, just remove the cover for the last 30 minutes or so of baking.

Recipe type: Side Dishes
Serves: 8
Prep time: 15 mins
Cook time: 6 hrs
Total time: 6 hrs 15 mins

OLD FASHIONED BAKED MAC & CHEESE

Ingredients

- 1 (7 ¼ oz.) pkg. Kraft macaroni and cheese dinner
- ¼ cup milk
- 1 (14 ½ oz.) can diced tomatoes, drained
- 1/4 cup Kraft Zesty Italian Dressing
- 2 Tbsp. butter, melted
- 1 cup crushed RITZ crackers (about 20 crackers)

Instructions

1. Preheat oven to 375 degrees.
2. Add macaroni to large saucepan of boiling water; cook until tender, drain.
3. Stir in milk and cheese sauce mix.
4. Pour into a greased 8-inch square baking dish.
5. Mix tomatoes and dressing.
6. Top macaroni mixture with tomato mixture.
7. Drizzle butter over cracker crumbs; toss with fork. Sprinkle over tomatoes.
8. Bake 15 minutes or until heated through and crumbs are golden.

Recipe type: Side Dishes
Serves: 12
Prep time: 20 mins
Cook time: 15 mins
Total time: 45 mins

PEGGY'S CORNBREAD DRESSING

"This is a good, old fashioned recipe for Southern-style dressing. You can serve this how you like, but we like it cut into squares. Some people would rather spoon it out, though. Whichever way you like is just as well. And if you like, you can also top it off with chicken gravy! Yum!" ~ *Mama Peggy*

Ingredients

- 1 small hen
- 4 cups cornbread (crumbled)
- 5 cups cold biscuits (crumbled)
- 4 stalks celery (chopped)
- 1 large or two medium onions, chopped
- Sage or poultry seasoning (to your personal taste - I like to taste it but not be overwhelmed by too much sage)
- Salt and pepper to taste
- 1 stick margarine
- 3 eggs, beaten
- 2 cans Cream of Chicken soup
- Chicken broth (to make dressing the texture of mashed potatoes)

Instructions

1. Sauté onions and celery in margarine until soft.
2. Crumble biscuits and cornbread in large bowl or pot.
3. Pour hot chicken broth over crumbs!

4. Add other ingredients, including one can of cream of chicken soup.
5. Let set about 1 hour to marinate.
6. If the mixture seems too dry, add a little more broth.
7. Pour mixture in 9x13-inch baking pan or dish!
8. Bake at 375 degrees for 30 or 45 minutes.
9. You may also mix chicken pieces in the dressing, if you like. Either way it's really good!

Recipe type: Side Dishes
Serves: 15
Prep time: 20 mins
Cook time: 45 mins
Total time: 1 hr 5 mins

PEGGY'S RESTAURANT COLE SLAW

This is the recipe for the legendary cole slaw from Peggy's Restaurant, which was served for almost 30 years on sandwiches and as a side dish in the family restaurant.

Ingredients

- ½ head cabbage
- 1 ½ medium carrots
- 1 medium sized bell pepper
- ½ Tbsp. course ground pepper
- ¼ Tbsp. fine ground pepper
- ¼ Tbsp. salt
- 1 ½ cup mayonnaise

Instructions

1. Strip the loose outer leaves from a medium sized cabbage and remove the core.
2. Quarter the cabbage to make it easier to shred.
3. Shred cabbage into a good-sized bowl using rough side of a grater, getting as much of the greener outer leaves as possible (it adds a little color to your slaw).
4. Cut the bell pepper into quarters and grate on top of cabbage, from the inside out. Grate to the skin, but don't grate in the skin of the bell pepper. You mainly want the meat of the bell pepper, not the skin.
5. Grate carrot on top of cabbage.

6. You should wind up with enough carrot and bell pepper to cover the cabbage you've already grated, but not so much that it heaps up.
7. Sprinkle mixture evenly with course ground pepper, find ground pepper and salt. My general rule is to shake each ingredient out as you move your hand quickly over the bowl, and then again as your hand comes back. That generally seems to be the right ratio. Do this for both kinds of pepper and salt.
8. Spoon your mayonnaise onto the mixture and mix.
9. You can mix everything with a spoon, but I've always done it with my hand. You'll quickly learn how to tell if there's enough mayonnaise by how dry the mixture feels to your hand.
10. Generally speaking, when the mixture is right, the slaw will be just moist enough to have a wee bit of standing liquid, but not so much as to be runny. Just moist.
11. And there you have it. Peggy's Restaurant cole slaw!

Recipe type: Side Dishes
Serves: 10-12
Prep time: 15 mins
Cook time: 15 mins
Total time: 30 mins

PEGGY'S RESTAURANT SANDWICH CHILI

This is the recipe for the legendary sandwich chili that Mama Peggy served-up on burgers and hotdogs at Peggy's Restaurant for almost 30 years. Folks in Kings Mountain, North Carolina, still talk about those burgers and hot dogs, and this chili was an essential ingredient.

Ingredients

- 1 lb. ground beef
- 2 Tbsp. minced onion
- 2 ½ Tbsp. chili powder
- 4 ½ Tbsp. ketchup
- ½ Tbsp. salt
- ½ Tbsp. pepper

Instructions

1. In saucepan over medium heat, brown ground beef.
2. Season with salt and pepper.
3. When beef is browned, drain grease if any.
4. Add in the rest of the ingredients and stir while mixture continues to cook, breaking down big chunks of meat into an even consistency.
5. Turn down to simmer for 15-20 minutes.
6. Salt and pepper to taste.

Recipe type: Side Dishes
Serves: 12
Prep time: 10 mins
Cook time: 20 mins
Total time: 30 mins

Slow Cooker Apple Butter

Here's a no-fuss recipe for delicious apple butter, which you can partly make overnight while you sleep. It's hard to beat good, old-fashioned slow-cooker apple butter.

Ingredients

- Apple slices
- ½ cup water
- 2 to 3 cup sugar
- ½ cup cider vinegar
- ½ tsp. ground cloves
- 2 tsp. cinnamon
- ½ tsp. allspice

Instructions

1. Fill a 4- to 5-quart slow cooker with your apple slices, pared and cored.
2. Add water.
3. Cook on low until the apples are tender.
4. If you wish, you can put this on at bedtime and let it cook all night.
5. Next morning, pour off all liquid.
6. Puree cook apples in a blender.

7. Return to slow cooker.
8. Add sugar, spices and vinegar. Cook for 3 hours or until it spreads consistently.
9. Makes 2 to 3 pints.

Recipe type: Side Dishes
Serves: 3 pints
Prep time: 30 mins
Cook time: 8 hrs
Total time: 8 hrs 30 mins

SOUTHERN STYLE COLLARD GREENS

Collard greens are such a regular part of traditional Southern diet that most cooks in the South don't realize that some people need a recipe for it. Well, here you go. Collard greens done in Southern style.

Ingredients

- 5 lbs. collard greens
- ½ lb. bacon
- ½ onion
- 2 Tbsp. apple cider vinegar
- Salt and pepper

Instructions

1. Soak greens in cold water several times to get rid of any grit.
2. Pull the tender leaves away from the stems and throw away the stems.

3. Cut bacon into bite size pieces and fry in a large stock pot.
4. Do not drain.
5. Add onion and cook until tender.
6. Add your collard greens (the pot will seem like it's overflowing, but the collards wilt).
7. Stir until collard have wilted (covering them every couple of minutes for a few minutes will help wilt them).
8. Add salt and pepper to taste and the vinegar.
9. Serve hot.

Recipe type: Side Dishes
Serves: 6
Prep time: 40 mins
Cook time: 30 mins
Total time: 1 hr 10 mins

SOUTHERN STYLE BUTTER BEANS

Any Southerner worth their salt has eaten so many butter beans in their lifetime it's hard to know whether to list it as a main dish or a side dish. If you haven't made a meal of butter beans over some fresh cornbread, you haven't spent much time in the South.

Ingredients

- 1 lb. bag of large lima beans
- Water to cover, plus an inch
- 1 cube chicken bouillon
- ¼ cup (½ stick) of butter

- 1 Tbsp. salt
- ¼ tsp. black pepper
- 4-6 cups of water

Instructions

1. Rinse and sort beans.
2. Place beans into stockpot with just enough water to cover them, plus about an inch.
3. Bring to a boil.
4. Cover and turn off the burner.
5. Let the beans soak covered for one hour, drain and set aside.
6. Pour 4-6 cups of fresh water over the beans.
7. Add chicken bouillon.
8. Bring to a boil, reduce heat to medium and let simmer for about 1 hour.
9. Stir in the butter
10. Continue cooking on a low simmer an additional hour to 1 hour and 30 minutes, or until beans are tender and sauce thickens.
11. Add additional chicken stock or water only if needed.

Recipe type: Side Dishes
Serves: 12
Prep time: 15 mins
Cook time: 2 hrs 30 mins
Total time: 2 hrs 45 mins

SPINACH-BACON MACARONI AND CHEESE

Ingredients

- 3 cups medium shell macaroni, uncooked
- 1 pkg. (6 oz.) fresh baby spinach leaves
- 4 slices bacon, chopped
- 2 Tbsp. flour
- 2 cups milk
- 2 cups Finely shredded sharp cheddar cheese
- ¼ cup grated Parmesan cheese

Instructions

1. Heat oven to 350 degrees.
2. Cook macaroni as directed on pkg., adding spinach for the last minute.
3. Cook bacon in large saucepan.
4. Remove bacon; save drippings in pan.
5. Add flour to drippings; cook and stir until bubbly.
6. Gradually stir in milk.
7. Bring to boil, stirring constantly; cook and stir 3 to 5 min. or until thickened.
8. Stir in 1 cup Cheddar and Parmesan; cook and stir until melted.
9. Add bacon and macaroni mixture; mix well.
10. Spoon into a 1½-quart casserole dish and top with the remaining cheddar.
11. Bake 20 minutes.

Recipe type: Side Dishes
Serves: 12
Prep time: 25 mins
Cook time: 20 mins
Total time: 45 mins

Peggy's Blog – My Encounter
May 22, 2011

Chico and I were just leisurely walking around our apartment building this morning! Leisurely means Chico was taking his own good time finding a suitable place to use the bathroom! I was just enjoying the beautiful day, looking at the flowers I had just potted the day before! Chico took me up one hill and down another! I was beginning to huff and puff by that time!

As we rounded the corner on the left side of the apartment, there was the cat who seems to play games with Chico. She'll wait until he gets almost nose to nose with her and then streak off so fast you can hardly see her! Then after taking a few more steps a second cat (my neighbor has been secretly feeding them) shot off behind the other cat! Suddenly Chico stopped dead in his tracks, then started off running! I started screaming for Chico to stop, because sitting there at a bush was a possum! Almost BABY possum! That cat had eaten all the skin off one side of her neck. It was sitting there, weaving as if hurt bad! My neighbor stuck her head out of her window and was yelling for Chico to stop because it had its mouth open as if to tell him "come on sucker", but it seemed to be staring right in my eyes, asking me to help it! I got Chico inside, by that time tears were stinging my eyes, because of the way that little possum was looking at me!

Lillian came out, retrieved a box from her car, cut holes in it so it could breathe, but when she got back out there, that little rascal had disappeared. I said, "Thank you Lord". Now I know anyone reading this would say "Heck, I would have killed it myself" but after being around my son Kevin all his life, and now Victoria, I could never have done such a thing! If I killed a spider he would say "Mama, he's just trying to find his way out of here". I would just shake my head and walk on!

This did remind me of something that happened way back fifty years ago! Loretta and I were double dating one Saturday night and back then you mostly just rode around or went to a Drive-in movie! Wasn't much else to do! We came through the Battleground Park road and came upon a strange looking critter sitting in the middle of the road! We said, "What in the world is that?????" They told us it was a possum! We were so fascinated with it because we had never seen a possum! I said, "Let's take it home" to Lo and she said "o.k." The boys got a box out of the trunk and put that possum in it and we brought it home. Mama and Daddy were already in bed, so we set it down in the dining room! When mama and daddy got up and saw that possum the roof nearly lifted! Daddy said, "You girls get that possum out of here and back where you got it and I mean NOW!" But there was one problem; the possum had gotten out of the box and we couldn't find it! We finally found it behind the refrigerator and down the road we went!

That was the first and last time I have ever seen a possum until today! I will still see those little black eyes looking at me! Wonder what the Vet would have said if I had carried that possum into his office?

Reminds me of another thing my old friend Mrs. Redmond told me one day! She has since died! She said her mother used to put possums in a cage to clean them out (in other words they would make sure what they ate for a few days or so) then she would boil them and serve them with sweet potatoes! She said her mother would call and invite my Grandfather to come to eat with them! She said "Man, your Granddaddy sure did love to eat that possum"!!!! I still shiver when I even think about that!!!!!

Maybe it will be another 50 years before I run up on a Possum! By that time I will be at home with Jesus! Do you reckon they have possums in Heaven?????

Soups & Stews

OLD-FASHIONED OYSTER STEW

This is just a good, simple oyster stew recipe. No muss, no fuss. And it's delicious!

Ingredients

- 2 cups milk
- 2 cups cream
- 1 pint oysters
- ¼ cup butter
- 2 tsp. salt
- ⅛ tsp. pepper

Instructions

1. In a 2 quart saucepan, scald the milk and cream.
2. Drain the oysters, but save the liquid for later.
3. Look over the oysters and make sure to remove any shell bits.
4. Melt the butter in saucepan.
5. Add the oysters with the liquid you saved.
6. Simmer for 3-4 minutes, or until the oysters have plumped up a bit and the edges have begun to curl.
7. Stir the oyster mixture into the scalded milk, and add the salt and pepper.

Recipe type: Soups & Stews
Serves: 6
Prep time: 10 mins
Cook time: 15 mins
Total time: 25 mins

PEGGY'S SALMON STEW

"I made this salmon stew last night! It was so good! Especially since the weather has turned chilly. I hope you will try it! My friend Libby puts onions in her salmon stew but I love mine! ENJOY!"
~ *Mama Peggy, Oct. 30, 2010*

Ingredients

- 1 large can Salmon (pink)
- 1 qt. milk
- 2 cans evaporated milk
- 1 stick margarine
- salt and pepper (to taste)
- Zesta saltine crackers

Instructions

1. In a large saucepan, combine milk, evaporated milk and margarine!
2. Remove skin and bones from Salmon and stir into milk.
3. Add salt and pepper.
4. Bring to a near boil.
5. Remove from heat.
6. Serve with crackers.
7. If you prefer more salmon, just add another can!

Recipe type: Soups & Stews
Serves: 6
Prep time: 10 mins
Cook time: 20 mins
Total time: 30 mins

Peggy's Blog – Christmas
December 22, 2011

Here we are again. Seems before we know it, another year has gone! THE YEAR OF OUR LORD'S BIRTH! I am proud to announce to the world that HE is my risen Lord and He has allowed me 78 yrs. to enjoy Christmas again and again! Ain't GOD good???

First, My Son and "Daughter" Victoria, who even if they live way down in Florida, fill my life with sunshine and joy with their phone calls and keeping in touch with me daily to see if I'm O.K. They keep me laughing about the antics of their cats and Kevin's pet squirrel! They have such great 'ol hearts, they would take in just about everything that had four legs and fur.

Then there's Michelle and Katie, who call me Grandma Peggy! They can never know how much that means to an ol' lady who has never had grandbabies of her own! (Thanks to Kevin LOL). From the first moment I walked into their mother's home these two sweet, kind girls opened their arms to me and made me feel so welcome! For the first time in my life, I felt complete and this was MY family! Thank you girls! I love you and can't thank you enough for being so good to me.

Then, My Sister Sue and her family, My brother Jack and My precious sister-in-law Helen and their family, then our baby sister Sherry (we called her 'Lil Iodine from an old comic strip – because being the baby, Mama spoiled her rotten, but she grew out of it (a lot)) and she's a great sister and her family. They are all there for me and I love them a lot!

My "sister" Kate, who fell and hurt herself pretty bad but is recovering nicely, thank you God again! I can't and won't ever forget my sister-in-law! She has always been a doll! She and my brother Robert married when they were just teenagers and I can't remember one Christmas that we didn't have a big box, filled with hair bows, coloring books and all sorts of things my parents couldn't afford! Bless you my Kate! I love you

Next, is my former Pastor Gene Land and his precious sidekick June! June didn't know what a lift she gave me this Christmas with the photos of the two of them! Twelve years together! Wow! Seems like yesterday I met Gene's bride for the first time and we seem to click! She is such a loving gal and she has taken such good care of my friend! I don't think Gene will ever know the influence he has on our family! We all loved him, and He was our Pastor, but he was our BROTHER! We still feel the same way! When any of us mention him, it's with such warmth! Like sunshine on a cloudy day! You hang in! Both of you! JOY COMES IN THE MORNING!!

Then last, all my friends at Kings Mountain Manor! I have such wonderful friends here! We stick up for each other! You wouldn't believe what comradeship we have here! Our most friend of all friends is a lady named Mary Helen Brown! She is constantly on the move, taking cards around to each apt. when someone is sick or just needs a friend! If you need her, she's there! She is also a great Christian girl! Also, my friend and adopted sister Libby! WE just look at each other sometimes and burst out laughing! We can't talk without laughing! I don't know what I would do without my Libby!

MERRY CHRISTMAS TO ALL MY BELOVED FRIENDS AND FAMILY!

I LOVE YOU ALL SO MUCH! HOPE TO BE AROUND NEXT CHRISTMAS!

IF NOT! YOU WILL KNOW WHERE I AM! GLORY TO GOD!!

~ Mama Peggy

Dressings, Salads & Spreads

CORNED BEEF SANDWICH SPREAD

"Absolutely delicious! This is one of my favorite recipes! My sister Loretta and I used to fix this spread often. Enjoy!" ~ *Mama Peggy*

Ingredients

- 1 Can Corned Beef
- 6 Hard-boiled eggs
- 2 medium onions
- 1 cup chopped sweet pickles
- 1 cup Duke's mayonnaise

Instructions

1. In processor, process the corned beef, eggs and onions.
2. Add pickles and mayonnaise.
3. It's the simplest thing in the world!

Recipe type: Dressings, Salads & Spreads
Serves: 12
Prep time: 10 mins
Cook time: 20 mins
Total time: 30 mins

WICASTA'S MIX LOW CARB DIPPING SAUCE

Ingredients

- 1 ½ cups Duke's mayonnaise
- 1 ½ cups country Dijon mustard (make sure it's zero carb)
- 3 Tbsp. ketchup
- 2 Tbsp. Stevia in the Raw

Instructions

1. In a large bowl, mix together the mayonnaise and the mustard until well blended.
2. Mix in ketchup until well blended.
3. Mix in Stevia until well blended.
4. Place in fridge after you're done, and use as needed, either as a dressing or a dipping sauce.

Recipe type: Dressings, Salads & Spreads
Serves: 24
Prep time: 15 mins
Cook time: 15 mins
Total time: 30 mins

PEGGY'S RANCH DRESSING

One of the most requested "recipes" people have asked about is Mama Peggy's recipe for ranch dressing. She didn't do anything fancy, but just used the Hidden Valley Original Ranch mix to make her dressing, mixed with buttermilk instead of milk. So, the secret to making your Ranch dressing taste like Mama Peggy's is to substitute buttermilk for the milk that the mix packets call for. And, of course, use Duke's mayonnaise if at all possible.

Ingredients

- 2 (1 oz.) packs Hidden Valley Original Ranch dressing mix
- 2 cups buttermilk
- 2 cups Duke's mayonnaise

Instructions

1. In a bowl, combine milk, mayonnaise and contents of mix packets.
2. Mix well.
3. Cover and refrigerate.
4. Chill 30 minutes to thicken.
5. Stir before serving.
6. Will yield enough to fill a 24 oz. salad dressing bottle.

Recipe type: Dressings, Salads & Spreads
Serves: 24
Prep time: 15 mins
Cook time: 15 mins
Total time: 30 mins

Peggy's Southern Style Home-Made Pimento Cheese

Pimento cheese has been called "the Pâté of The South". Pimento cheese is such a big part of Southern culture that Southerners are shocked to learn that folks in other parts of the country have never heard of it.

Ingredients

- ½ lb. Kraft's sharp cheddar cheese
- ½ lb. Kraft's medium cheddar cheese
- 2 cups Duke's mayonnaise
- 4 oz. Dromedary diced pimientos
- 1 tsp. salt
- 1 tsp. course ground pepper
- ½ tsp. garlic salt

Instructions

1. Grate cheese into a large bowl.
2. Add mayonnaise and mix well.
3. Add salt, pepper and garlic, mix well.
4. Add pimientos with juice and mix well.
5. If the taste is to your liking, you're done. Just put the pimento cheese in the fridge for a few hours or overnight. It's a lot better when the flavors have had some time to "marry".

Recipe type: Dressings, Salads & Spreads
Serves: 20
Prep time: 20 mins
Cook time: 20 mins
Total time: 40 mins

SOUTHERN CHICKEN SALAD

You see a lot of recipes for chicken salad on the Internet, but the images that go with 'em all look like they've been made by some chef at a fancy restaurant in New York City. The one thing Southern cooks know to do to make great food is to keep it simple. And this Southern chicken salad recipe is exactly what's called for if you want a no-fuss chicken salad for eating. There's no point in getting fancy. If you make this chicken salad, it won't be around long enough to impress the neighbors.

Ingredients

- 3 cup cooked & diced chicken (1 young chicken)
- 1 cup Duke's mayonnaise
- ½ cup finely chopped celery (about 1½ stalks)
- ½ tsp. salt
- ½ tsp. course ground pepper
- ½ Tbsp. lemon juice

Instructions

1. Cook 1 young chicken.
2. When done, remove chicken from heat and allow to cool.
3. Once chicken is cool enough to handle, remove meat from the bone, picking out the best bits. You should come up with about 3 cups of chicken.
4. Dice chicken, chop celery and mix all of the ingredients well.
5. Salt and pepper to taste (I sometimes use a little more salt than what's called for).
6. Store covered in refrigerator and allow to "marry".
7. Can be made 1 to 2 days in advance so flavors can blend.

Recipe type: Dressings, Salads & Spreads
Serves: 6-8
Prep time: 30 mins
Cook time: 1 hr
Total time: 1 hr 30 mins

Addendum

THE CHANEY BUNCH

Rev. Robert Lattie Chaney
Mar 1, 1895 – Nov 8, 1959
m.
Winnie Victoria Moss
Feb 8, 1895 – Mar 25, 1967

Children:

Maudie Lucille Chaney Gladden
Edith Isabel Chaney Millwood
Grady Lee Chaney
Robert Howard Chaney
Doretha Odell "Sis" Chaney
John Lee Chaney
Martha Sue Chaney Rhea
Jack Douglas Chaney
Peggy Joyce Chaney
Loretta Lee Chaney
Sherry Jean Chaney Short

Peggy's Restaurant
1992 Menu, Page 1

SANDWICHES AND BURGERS

Hamburger (Mustard, Chili & Onions)..................................$1.45
Cheeseburger (Lettuce & Tomato) $1.60
Bacon Cheeseburger (Lettuce & Tomato)............................$2.25
Large Hamburger (Mustard, Chili & Onions).......................$2.10
Large Cheeseburger (Lettuce & Tomato)............................$2.25
Large Bacon Cheeseburger (Lettuce & Tomato)..................$2.90
Hotdog (Mustard, Chili & Onions) $1.10
Chicken Fillet (Lettuce & Tomato) $2.10
Chuck Wagon Steak (Lettuce & Tomato) $2.10
Bacon, Lettuce & Tomato $1.60
Ham, Lettuce & Tomato $1.85
Ham & Cheese...$1.85
Grilled Cheese...$1.10
Country Ham (Plain)..$2.10
Country Ham (Lettuce & Tomato)......................................$2.40
Fishwich (Plain) $1.45
Fishwich (Cheese & Tartar Sauce)......................................$1.60
Devilled Egg (Homemade) $1.40

BASKETS (French Fries & Side Order of Slaw)

Regular Burger $2.45
Regular Cheeseburger...$2.65
Whopper Burger..$3.10
Whopper Cheeseburger...$3.30
Ham & Cheese (Lettuce & Tomato) $3.10
Chicken Nuggets $3.10
Chuck Wagon Steak..$3.10
Hotdog Basket..$2.10

Peggy's Restaurant
1992 Menu, Page 1 continued

SIDE ORDERS

French Fries	$1.00
Onion Rings	$1.00
Apple Sticks	$1.00
Vegetable Sticks	$1.00
Regular Tossed Salad	$1.35
Chef Salad	$3.00

Of course, at Peggy's,
You can always get your burger made any way you want it.
Have something special in mind?
Just ask us.

PEGGY'S RESTAURANT
1992 MENU, PAGE 2

SPECIALS

Fried Chicken (Dark Meat)	$4.75
Fried Chicken (White Meat)	$5.00
Chicken Fillet	$4.75
Chicken Livers	$4.75
Chicken Tenders	$5.00
Flounder	$4.75
Catfish Strips	$4.75
Shrimp	$5.25
Veal Cutlet	$4.75
Chuck Wagon Steak	$4.75
Pepper Steak	$4.75
Hamburger Steak	$5.00
Baked Ham	$4.75
Country Ham	$5.25
All Vegetable Plate	$0.90

(Price is per vegetable. Drink is not included with vegetable plate)

Your choice of three vegetables comes with our plates.
Choose from the list below,
or see the Daily Special section for the daily vegetables.

Cole Slaw	Apple Sauce
Pickled Beets	Apple Sticks
Tossed Salad	Vegetable Sticks
Sliced Tomatoes	French Fries
Cottage Cheese	Hashbrowns
(with Peaches)	Onion Rings

Peggy's Restaurant
1992 Menu, Page 2 continued

PIE…….. $0.70
Lemon Meringue
Chocolate Meringue

THANK YOU – PLEASE COME SEE US AGAIN!

PEGGY'S RESTAURANT

Index

Table of Contents iv
Introduction 1
Peggy's Blog – Mama's Birthday 7
Main Dishes 9
    Baked Chicken Breasts 10
    Basic Best Salmon Loaf 11
    Crouton Breaded Chicken 12
    Chicken & Dumplings 14
    (My sister Edith's recipe) 14
    Quick Chicken and Dumplings 15
    Chicken Lickin' Pork Chops 17
    Creamy Cheese Grits and Spinach 18
    Crock Pot Beef Stew 19
    Crock-Pot Chicken 20
    Fresh Corn Cakes 21
    Fried Chicken Strips 22
    My Mama's Salmon Patties 24
    Old Fashioned Meatloaf 25
    Old Fashioned Roast Turkey 26
    Pepper Steak 28
    Salisbury Steak 29
    Slow Cooked Barbecue Pork 31

    Southern Stewed Potatoes 32

    Spinach Lasagna Roll-Ups 35

    Stuffed Bell Peppers... 37

Peggy's Blog – Dear Lo.. 39

Casseroles 41

    Baked Corn Casserole 42

    Baked Macaroni with Tomato & Cheese 43

    Beef Noodle Casserole 44

    Black Eyed Pea Casserole 46

    Broccoli Mac & Cheese Bake 47

    Chicken Cheese & Rice Casserole 49

    Chicken and Rice Casserole... 50

    Chicken Salad Casserole 51

    Corned Beef Casserole 52

    Creamy Chicken and Rice Bake 53

    Crockpot Chicken and Rice Casserole 54

    Easy Chicken & Biscuits 55

    Easy Chicken Pot Pie 56

    Ground Beef and Potato Casserole... 57

    Homestyle Green Bean Casserole 59

    King Ranch Chicken Casserole.. 61

    Mexican Chicken Casserole.. 63

    Peggy's Broccoli Casserole 64

    Peggy's Pinto Bean Casserole 65

Pork Chop Potato Bake Casserole	67
Sweet Potato Casserole	68
Squash Casserole	69
That's Na-Cho Casserole!	70
Vegetable Casserole	72
Vidalia Onion Casserole	73

Peggy's Blog – In Church Again 74

Gravy 76

Chicken Gravy	77
Chocolate Gravy	78
Peggy's Breakfast Gravy	79

Peggy's Blog – You Can't Go Home Again! 81

Appetizers 83

Ann's Oven-Roasted Potatoes	84
Cheese Ball 1	85
Cheese Ball 2	86
Cheesy Spinach and Bacon Dip	87
Chocolate Chip Cheese Ball	88
Crab Dip	89
Deviled Cheese Puffs	89
Olive Cheese Ball	91
Peggy's Restaurant Livermush Biscuit	92
Sausage Dip	94
Spinach Balls	95

Peggy's Blog – A Drastic Decision 96
Beverages 98
    Homemade Eggnog 99
    Peach Tea Sangria 101
    Peggy's Southern Style Sweet Tea 102
    Strawberry Tea 104
Peggy's Blog – The Christmas Spirit 105
Bread 108
    Peggy's Cornbread 109
    Peggy's Southern Style Buttermilk Biscuits 110
    Pumpkin Bread 112
Peggy's Blog – Happy New Year! 114
Desserts - Cakes 117
    Apple, Walnut, and Honey Spice Cake 118
    Applesauce Cake 120
    Carrot Layer Cake 121
    Cold Oven Pound Cake 123
    Dream Cake 124
    Old-Fashioned Black Walnut Pound Cake 125
    Old Fashioned Lemon Pound Cake 127
    Orange Crush Pound Cake 128
    Peanut Butter Chocolate Cake 130
    Pineapple Coconut Cake 132
    Pineapple Coconut Layer Cake 134

- Pumpkin Pecan Cake 135
- Southern Pineapple Pound Cake 137
- Sweet Potato Pound Cake 138

Peggy's Blog – Loretta, My Best Friend 140

Desserts - Candy & Cookies 145
- Cathedral Windows Candy 146
- Double Chocolate Peanut Butter Bars 147
- Dulce De Leche Bars 149
- Macadamia Macaroons 150
- Peanut Butter Fudge 152
- Peanut Butter Rice Krispie Treats 153
- Pecan Pie Bars 154

Peggy's Blog – Valentine's Day 156

Desserts - Pies 159
- Baked Chocolate Pie 160
- Best Pecan Pie 161
- Cherry Pie 162
- Cinnamon Streusel Sweet Potato Pie 163
- Coconut Pie 165
- Crumb, Apple and Pumpkin Pie 166
- Crunch Top Peach Pie 168
- French Silk Chocolate Pie 169
- Million Dollar Pie 171
- Old Fashioned Golden Apple Pie 172

Peanut Butter Pie 173

Pinto Bean Pie 175

Pumpkin Pie 176

Ritz Cracker Pecan Pie 177

Strawberry Pie 178

Sweet Potato Pie 179

Teresa's Cream Pie 181

Wonderful Lemon Pie 182

Peggy's Blog – Woodpecker! 184

Desserts – Pudding & Other 186

   Cherry Supreme Dessert 187

   Gingerbread Pumpkin Trifle 188

   Coconut Rice Pudding 190

   Homemade Vanilla Pudding 191

   Ice Cream Cake 193

   Lucille's Christmas Icebox Fruit Cake 194

   Maple Walnut Sticky Buns 195

   My Mama's Bread Pudding 197

   Never Fail Meringue 198

   Old Fashioned Snow Cream 200

   Orange Fluff Salad 201

   Peggy's Apple Crumble Pie Cobbler 202

   Peggy's Banana Pudding 204

   Running Towards Chocolate 205

Strawberry Cobbler 207

Strawberry Fruit Salad 208

Strawberry Pudding 209

Peggy's Blog – Sunshine and Warm Weather 211

Side Dishes 213

Fried Okra 214

Hush Puppies 215

Italian Potato Salad 216

Low Carb Baked Veggie Cheese Squares 218

Old Fashioned Baked Beans 220

Old Fashioned Baked Mac & Cheese 222

Peggy's Cornbread Dressing 223

Peggy's Restaurant Cole Slaw 225

Peggy's Restaurant Sandwich Chili 227

Slow Cooker Apple Butter 228

Southern Style Collard Greens 229

Southern Style Butter Beans 230

Spinach-Bacon Macaroni and Cheese 232

Peggy's Blog – My Encounter 234

Soups & Stews 237

Old-Fashioned Oyster Stew 238

Peggy's Salmon Stew 239

Peggy's Blog – Christmas 241

Dressings, Salads & Spreads 244

- Corned Beef Sandwich Spread 245
- Wicasta's Mix Low Carb Dipping Sauce 246
- Peggy's Ranch Dressing 247
- Peggy's Southern Style Home-Made Pimento Cheese 248
- Southern Chicken Salad 249

Addendum 251
- The Chaney Bunch 251
- Peggy's Restaurant 1992 Menu, Page 1 252
- Peggy's Restaurant 1992 Menu, Page 1 continued 253
- Peggy's Restaurant 1992 Menu, Page 2 254
- Peggy's Restaurant 1992 Menu, Page 2 continued 255

My Recipes 264

My Recipes

My Recipes

My Recipes

My Recipes

My Recipes

My Recipes

My Recipes

My Recipes

My Recipes

My Recipes

"Well done, good and faithful servant!"
~ Matthew 25:23

Peggy Joyce Chaney

May 11, 1933 – Dec 30, 2011

www.ingramcontent.com/pod-product-compliance
Lightning Source LLC
Chambersburg PA
CBHW030309080526
44584CB00012B/502